LONGMAN LITERATURE

Voices of the Great War

Selected and edited by Geoff Barton

New Longman Literature
Post-1914 Fiction

Susan Hill *I'm the King of the Castle* 0 582 22173 0
       The Woman in Black 0 582 02660 1
       The Mist in the Mirror 0 582 25399 3
Aldous Huxley *Brave New World* 0 582 06016 8
Robin Jenks *The Cone-Gatherers* 0 582 06017 6
Doris Lessing *The Fifth Child* 0 582 06021 4
Joan Lindsay *Picnic at Hanging Rock* 0 582 08174 2
Bernard MacLaverty *Lamb* 0 582 06557 7
Brian Moore *Lies of Silence* 0 582 08170 X
George Orwell *Animal Farm* 0 582 06010 9
F Scott Fitzgerald *The Great Gatsby* 0 582 06023 0
Robert Swindells *Daz 4 Zoe* 0 582 30243 9
Anne Tyler *A Slipping-Down Life* 0 582 29247 6
Virginia Woolf *To the Lighthouse* 0 582 09714 2

Post-1914 Short Stories

Angelou, Goodison, Senior & Walker *Quartet of Stories* 0 582 28730 8
Stan Barstow *The Human Element and Other Stories* 0 582 23369 0
Roald Dahl *A Roald Dahl Selection* 0 582 22281 8
selected by Geoff Barton *Stories Old and New* 0 582 28931 9
selected by Madhu Bhinda *Stories from Africa* 0 582 25393 4
       Stories from Asia 0 582 03922 3
selected by Celeste Flower *Mystery and Horror* 0 582 28928 9
selected by Jane Christopher *War Stories* 0 582 28927 0
selected by Susan Hill *Ghost Stories* 0 582 02261 X
selected by Beverley Naidoo, *Global Tales* 0 582 28929 7
Christine Donovan & Alun Hicks
selected by Andrew Whittle & *Ten D H Lawrence Short Stories* 0 582 29249 2
Roy Blatchford

Post-1914 Poetry

collected & edited by Roy Blatchford *Voices of the Great War* 0 582 29248 4
edited by George MacBeth *Poetry 1900-1975* 0 582 35149 9
edited by Julia Markus & Paul Jordan *Poems 2* 0 582 25401 9

Post-1914 Plays

Alan Ayckbourn *Absent Friends* 0 582 30242 0
Terrence Rattigan *The Winslow Boy* 0 582 06019 2
Jack Rosenthal *P'Tang, Yang, Kipperbang and other TV Plays* 0 582 22389 X
Willy Russell *Educating Rita* 0 582 06013 3
       Shirley Valentine 0 582 08173 4
selected by Geoff Barton *Ten Short Plays* 0 582 25383 7
selected by Michael Marland *Scenes from Plays* 0 582 25394 2
Peter Shaffer *The Royal Hunt of the Sun* 0 582 06014 1
       Equus 0 582 09712 6
Bernard Shaw *Pygmalion* 0 582 06015 X
       Saint Joan 0 582 07786 9
Sheridan, Richard Brinsley *The Rivals/The School for Scandal* 0 582 25396 9

Contents

Later voices 24

CONTENTS

CONTENTS

Introduction

Summer 1914

Everyone agreed that the summer of 1914 was remarkable. Long hot days and bright skies followed one another – ideal weather for outdoor swimming, country walks, picnics, and lolling on deckchairs. It could only be described as perfect.

Siegfried Sassoon played county cricket. Robert Graves went climbing in the Welsh mountains. Edmund Blunden went on country walks around Oxford and worked on his poetry. And Wilfred Owen, near Bordeaux, taught English to the boys of a French family.

On August 4 a new day broke over Europe. In France, the sun rose over the cornfields and the lush pastureland surrounding the rivers Somme and Ancre. Two hundred and fifty miles away in London people pulled back their curtains on a glorious Bank Holiday Monday morning. Saturday and Sunday had been slightly disappointing – muggy, airless, sometimes overcast. This morning it was obvious that it would be a wonderful day.

As they hurried their breakfasts and packed picnic things, few would have noticed the tiny advertisement placed in the personal columns of the morning newspapers:

GERMAN MOBILISATION

Germans who have served, or who are liable to serve, are requested to return to Germany without delay, as best they can. For information they can apply to the German Consulate, Russell Square, London WC.

RL Von Ranke. Consul.

In general the newspapers were full of gloom. Germany had declared war on Russia, invaded Luxembourg and was on the brink of invading Belgium. The evening editions would report that Germany had declared war on France. But crisis or no crisis, today was a holiday, and across Britain crowds flooded towards the seaside and the country.

Hints of war

At London's railway stations people arrived to find that all holiday excursions were cancelled. The trains were needed for soldiers. At Waterloo, the station was teeming with Royal Naval Reservists who had been officially mobilised. Great crowds gathered to watch, and as they watched, they sang: 'All the Nice Girls Love a Sailor' and 'Rule Britannia'. The trains intended for day-trippers left packed with sailors bound for Portsmouth. The crowds cheered them off and waved enthusiastically.

At Victoria Station there was less enthusiasm. This was where the boat-trains left from, bound for the continent. Battered suitcases and hastily packed bags were strewn around, as cooks and waiters and barbers and butchers made for the third-class carriages. These were the German workers of London, heeding the message of the morning papers, and quickly returning home.

And so the sun shone. People headed for the London parks, and for the zoo. There was an Anglo-American Exhibition at White City with exciting scenes from the Wild West. Madame Tussaud's waxworks did a roaring trade as people queued to look at the life-like images of the day's famous names: Their Majesties King George and Queen Mary, His Imperial Majesty The Emperor of Austria, His Majesty King Peter of Serbia.

All through the day, beneath the laughter and the cheering and the sandwiches and the sun, a single question lingered in people's minds. Would Britain go to war with Germany? On that day, the

British Government had sent a message to the German Government saying that it would not tolerate any military action against Belgium, that such an act would bring about retaliation.

By four o'clock on Bank Holiday Monday everybody knew. One hundred thousand telegrams were sent out by the army, guaranteed delivery anywhere in Britain within the hour. They contained a single word: 'Mobilise'. Britain was at war with Germany.

Early days

At home, the early days of the War were dominated by optimistic newspaper headlines.

FOUR DAYS BATTLE – A BRILLIANT SERIES OF ENGAGEMENTS

GERMAN ONSLAUGHT – HOW THE BRITISH KEPT THEM BACK

Posters appeared reminding people at home to 'do their bit':

Five questions to patriotic shopkeepers:

1. Have you any fit men between 19 and 38 years of age serving behind your counter who at this moment ought to be serving their country?

2. Will you call your male employees together and explain to them that in order to end the War quickly we must have more men?

3. Will you tell them what you are prepared to do for them whilst they are fighting for the Empire?

4. Have you realised that we cannot have 'business as usual' whilst the War continues?

THE ARMY WANTS <u>MORE MEN TO-DAY</u>

5. Could not women or older men fill their places till the War is over?

YOUR COUNTRY WILL APPRECIATE YOUR HELP
God Save the King

Innocent optimism

On the whole men queued to play their part in the War. Look at the bright faces on those early photographs – men in caps and dark clothes smiling as they wait to sign up, 'as if it were all an August Bank Holiday lark,' as Philip Larkin says.

This mood of innocent optimism – surely the War would be over by Christmas – is reflected in a tiny, sad note in the *Times* of August 9, 1914:

> At an inquest on the body of Arthur Sydney Evelyn Annesley, aged 49, formerly a captain in the Rifle Brigade, who committed suicide by flinging himself under a heavy van at Pimlico, the Coroner stated that worry caused by the feeling that he was not going to be accepted for service led him to take his life.

Those in the army crossed the Channel in ships and boats. In France, trains left the Channel ports every ten minutes, carrying the soldiers to a small corner that would become the concentrated battle-zone of the War. On board the trains, the carnival atmosphere continued: bright weather outside, trains pulling through lush countryside, picnics of cheese, ham and boiled eggs, songs and laughter and cheers.

War and language

At the end of the train rides, there were long marches through villages and up lanes, and still-optimistic soldiers were reassured by the ringing words of their commanders:

> *Our cause is just. We are called upon to fight beside our gallant allies in France and Belgium in no war of arrogance, but to uphold our national honour, independence and freedom. We have violated no neutrality, nor have we been false to any treaties. We enter upon this conflict with the clearest consciousness that we are fighting for right and honour.*

> *Having then this trust in the righteousness of our cause, pride in the glory of our military traditions, and belief in the efficiency of our army, we go forward together to do or die for*
>
> GOD – KING – AND COUNTRY
>
> (Sir John French)

Right, honour, pride, glory, traditions . . . the language is powerfully persuasive, emotive, full of echoes of a bygone era. It was language that belonged to Victorian times and which was the only possible language of the early literature of the War. Critic Paul Fussell highlights this in his 'table of equivalents':

A friend is a	*comrade*
Friendship is	*comradeship or fellowship*
The dead on the battlefield are	*the fallen*
Danger is	*peril*
One's death is one's	*fate*
Not to complain is to be	*manly*
The sky is the	*heavens*

Some officers would often talk in these terms, with the War described as if it were a great and glorious game of football, rugby or cricket. Leading his men into one of the most devastating battles of the War, the Somme, one officer actually treated it in this way, as a survivor recalls:

> *As the gun-fire died away I saw an infantryman climb onto the parapet into No Man's Land, beckoning others to follow. As he did so he kicked off a football. A good kick. The ball rose and travelled well towards the German line. That seemed to be the signal to advance.*

Captain Nevill was killed instantly. Two of the footballs are preserved in the British Museum. Twenty thousand men were killed on the first day of the attack; 600,000 would lose their lives in the four-month campaign.

Never such innocence again. Hopes that the War would be a brisk affair quickly crumbled. Within three months of its start, it had become locked into the shape it would take for the next four years: trench stalemate.

Life in the trenches

The First World War was fought from trenches – long lines of dug-outs slicing across France and Belgium. As Paul Fussell says in **The Great War and Modern Memory**, 'theoretically it would have been possible to walk from Belgium to Switzerland entirely below ground'. He calculates that there must have been around 25,000 miles of trenches, sufficient to encircle the earth.

During the course of the War the position of these trenches remained fairly fixed, occasionally moving forward or back a few hundred metres and – very occasionally – a few miles. The front line trench was where the battles were launched: you went over the top and across the No Man's Land that lay between you and the enemy. It might be a distance of fifty metres to a mile. It would be strewn with barbed wire, a recent American invention for restraining animals which was used heavily during the First World War.

A front line or firing trench was six to eight feet deep. On the side towards the enemy it was built up with earth or sandbags perhaps a metre higher. There would be a fire-step, two feet high. You stood on this to shoot or throw grenades. A good trench would zigzag, to make it stronger (only part of it could then collapse at any one time) and to make it safer (the enemy would only be able to fire a limited distance along it). It would have wooden duck-boards along the bottom. Your trench would be continuously crumbling and need rebuilding. It would also continuously fill with water. But this was your home, and you invented trench nick-names, like Piccadilly, Regent Street and the Strand.

Conditions

An exhibition at Kensington Gardens early in the War showed people at home what the trenches were like, described as a place of 'refreshment and repose'. Wilfred Owen visited it and said the exhibition was 'the laughing stock of the army'. The reality of trench life was far more grim. Your trench was cold and wet and badly constructed. Pervading the air was the smell of rum and blood. By day you cleaned weapons, repaired trenches, found the lice in your clothes and popped them between your fingers.

You fought against the damp too. You lived where the water-table and the rainfall rate were high. Trenches frequently flooded several feet deep. As a matter of routine you wore waders or thigh boots. Pumps worked night and day, with little effect. As Wilfred Owen wrote to his mother in 1917:

> The waders are of course indispensable. In $2^1/_2$ miles of trench which I waded yesterday there was not one inch of dry ground. There is a mean depth of two feet of water.

(Collected Letters)

And then, of course, there were the rats – bloated, muddy and bold. They fed on dead flesh, of humans and horses. Sometimes, for amusement, you shot at them or coshed them. But they haunted you with terrifying courage, as one soldier recalls:

> We are fairly plagued with rats. They have eaten nearly everything in the mess, including the tablecloth and the operation orders! We borrowed a large cat and shut it up at night to exterminate them, and found the place empty next morning. The rats must have eaten it up, bones, fur, and all and dragged it to their holes.

(P. H. Pilditch)

This was the daily horror of war – imprisoned in a muddy grave – and then at night the battles would begin.

Facing the horrors

How can human beings hope to come to terms with experiences like these? A few weeks ago you might have been enjoying the

English summer. Now you had to live like this. No wonder in the Great War you lived for letters – your link not only with the people at home but with normality, with a world that made sense. And you wrote – letters, diaries, poems, journals – anything to help you come to terms with the experiences of the trenches. Writing like this can serve an important purpose, allowing us to shape and organise our thoughts, feelings and fears.

Imaginative literature in this way serves a different purpose from factual information. As an example, consider the facts surrounding just one battle:

July 1916: Battle of the Somme

Previous assaults on the German lines had been disastrous. At the First Battle of the Marne in 1914, 500,000 casualties on both sides. By mid-November, at the First Battle of Ypres, most of the original British army were wiped out. The Second Battle of Ypres, in 1915, saw the first use of poison gas. British casualties: 60,000. In September 1915, at the Battle of Loos, the British experimented with chlorine gas, most of which was blown back into British trenches. The assault was called off after 11 days. Cost: 60,000 more British casualties. January 1916: Conscription introduced. Lord Derby's 'scheme' was recognition that volunteers would not provide sufficient numbers. For people at home, it was a visible sign of how things were going wrong.

British commanders decide that a huge assault on the enemy is required – to break the deadlock of the War, and to restore the morale of the troops and at home. This huge attack on the German forces around the River Somme is meticulously planned and begins with the shelling of German lines. One and a half million shells are fired during a week-long bombardment. Then the attacking waves of British troops walk out of their trenches into No Man's Land. The German soldiers watch in amazement as the enemy walks out into uncut wire. From the safety of their parapets they fire. Sixty thousand are killed or wounded on this first day. Twenty thousand bodies lie virtually unreachable in No Man's Land. It took days until the wounded stopped crying out.

What dimension can imaginative literature – stories, novels, plays and poetry – bring to unimaginable horrors like this?

War and literature

Literature takes a situation we can barely hope to imagine and enables us to experience it. This is the real achievement of the writers contained in this collection. They use language to express the personal suffering of a war that swallowed up millions of lives. Walk into almost any church in almost any town or village in Britain, France or Germany and you will see a memorial to the men of the Great War – a list of names of people who belonged to families, their friends and workmates. The writers of the Great War speak on behalf of them all.

Sometimes we treat texts as if they exist in isolation. We pick up a story or poem; we read it and discuss its characters, themes and language. We treat it as self-contained. The point about the War poets is that they wrote directly from a historical experience, frequently hunched over candles, writing in notebooks and on scraps of paper. To understand fully their work, we need to know about the historical context – which is why much of this introduction is devoted to illuminating the background.

But it is important to remember that the poets are not merely reporters of the war. Their writing does not have the same purpose as, for example, the diaries and letters contained in this collection. Several of the poets write about specific battles and assaults – Wilfred Owen's 'Exposure', Edmund Blunden's 'Third Ypres', for example. But they aren't simply giving us the statistics of a battle, like the facts listed above for the Battle of the Somme. They make us relive it through one person's eyes.

The reason that this is important is that the poets of the First

World War have swung in and out of fashion throughout this century. After brief popularity following the War, they were neglected until the Second World War, and then again until the 1960s. Now they are recognised as an important part of the English literary heritage. But there is a problem. Because these writers are so closely connected with a major event, it can be difficult to take our focus away from the content – what they describe – and look objectively at their language. The great War poets – Sassoon, Rosenberg, Owen and Blunden – not only deepen our understanding of the conditions of the War. They also changed the language of poetry.

Look at the 'Early voices' section of this collection (page 1). Not only the attitudes but also the vocabulary seem to belong to an earlier age. In Sassoon and Owen, in the 'Later voices' section (page 24), poetry and the twentieth century coincide. The formal, polite conventions of late Victorian and Georgian poetry were blown apart by the experimental work of these writers. In the trenches, responding to the unimaginable, they forged a language which was capable of capturing the realities of what they saw and felt.

In other words, these writers have an important literary status – moving literature on and paving the way for the experimental styles that followed the War – of writers like T. S. Eliot, James Joyce and Ezra Pound – as well as recording the human dimension of life in the War.

Neglected voices

Other voices of the First World War have frequently been neglected – in particular, the poetry of women and poets from overseas. This collection aims to represent the full emotional picture of the War by giving them a voice, as well as by providing other texts with other viewpoints. So you will find propaganda from the War, speeches, leaflets, letters and diaries, and three powerful fictional extracts (pages 79–116). This is followed by photographs which will give you a vivid idea of conditions for the men in the trenches. All of these are intended to enhance our understanding of the Great War. But the writings also serve another purpose: to show the power of different literary forms to make an event of almost a century ago come hauntingly and disturbingly alive.

I hope that **Voices of the Great War** fascinates, disturbs, informs and inspires you, and that you gain a deeper understanding of the events and language that created these remarkable texts and their remarkable writers.

Geoff Barton

■ Early voices

These early voices present a view of the Great War which was extremely well received in their day, but which can now seem sickly or sentimental in comparison with the harsher writings of the poets who followed. Nevertheless, they represent an important perspective on the First World War.

Thomas Hardy (1840–1928)

Thomas Hardy is often described as a nineteenth-century novelist and twentieth-century poet. In fact, poetry was always his first love and, after the increasingly critical reactions to his fiction, he abandoned novel-writing in 1896 to concentrate on poetry. As a poet, he is most famous today for his remarkable and moving 'Poems of 1912–13', written in memory of his first wife, Emma. He remarried in 1914, the year when the War broke out, and a number of his poems reflect his distress at the events.

Channel Firing

That night your great guns, unawares,
Shook all our coffins as we lay,
And broke the chancel window-squares,
We thought it was the Judgment-day

And sat upright. While drearisome
Arose the howl of wakened hounds:
The mouse let fall the altar-crumb
The worms drew back into the mounds,

The glebe cow drooled. Till God called, 'No;
It's gunnery practice out at sea
Just as before you went below;
The world is as it used to be:

'All nations striving strong to make
Red war yet redder. Mad as hatters
They do no more for Christés sake
Than you who are helpless in such matters.

'That this is not the judgment-hour
For some of them's a blessed thing,
For if it were they'd have to scour
Hell's floor for so much threatening . . .

'Ha, ha. It will be warmer when
I blow the trumpet (if indeed
I ever do; for you are men,
And rest eternal sorely need).'

So down we lay again. 'I wonder,
Will the world ever saner be,'
Said one, 'than when He sent us under
In our indifferent century!'

And many a skeleton shook his head.
'Instead of preaching forty year,'
My neighbour Parson Thirdly said,
'I wish I had stuck to pipes and beer.'

Again the guns disturbed the hour,
Roaring their readiness to avenge,
As far inland as Stourton Tower,
And Camelot, and starlit Stonehenge.

April 1914

Men Who March Away
(Song of the Soldiers)

What of the faith and fire within us
    Men who march away
    Ere the barn-cocks say
    Night is growing gray,
Leaving all that here can win us;
What of the faith and fire within us
    Men who march away?

Is it a purblind prank, O think you,
    Friend with the musing eye,
    Who watch us stepping by
    With doubt and dolorous sigh?
Can much pondering so hoodwink you!
Is it a purblind prank, O think you,
    Friend with the musing eye?

Nay. We well see what we are doing,
    Though some may not see –
    Dalliers as they be –
    England's need are we;
Her distress would leave us rueing:
Nay. We well see what we are doing,
    Though some may not see!

In our heart of hearts believing
 Victory crowns the just,
 And that braggarts must
 Surely bite the dust,
Press we to the field ungrieving,
In our heart of hearts believing
 Victory crowns the just.

Hence the faith and fire within us
 Men who march away
 Ere the barn-cocks say
 Night is growing gray,
Leaving all that here can win us;
Hence the faith and fire within us
 Men who march away.

5 September 1914

The Dead and the Living One

The dead woman lay in her first night's grave,
And twilight fell from the clouds' concave,
And those she had asked to forgive forgave.

The woman passing came to a pause
By the heaped white shapes of wreath and cross,
And looked upon where the other was.

And as she mused there thus spoke she:
'Never your countenance did I see,
But you've been a good good friend to me!'

Rose a plaintive voice from the sod below:
'O woman whose accents I do not know,
What is it that makes you approve me so?'

'O dead one, ere my soldier went,
I heard him saying, with warm intent,
To his friend, when won by the blandishment:

'"I would change for that lass here and now!
And if I return I may break my vow
To my present Love, and contrive somehow

'"To call my own this new-found pearl,
Whose eyes have the light, whose lips the curl
I always have looked for in a girl!"

'– And this is why that by ceasing to be –
Though never your countenance did I see –
You prove you a good good friend to me;

'And I pray each hour for your soul's repose
In gratitude for your joining those
No lover will clasp when his campaigns close.'

Away she turned, when arose to her eye
A martial phantom of gory dye,
That said, with a thin and far-off sigh:

'O sweetheart, neither shall I clasp you!
For the foe this day has pierced me through,
And sent me to where she is. Adieu! –

'And forget not when the night-wind's whine
Calls over this turf where her limbs recline,
That it travels on to lament by mine.'

There was a cry by the white-flowered mound,
There was a laugh from underground,
There was a deeper gloom around.

1915

A New Year's Eve in War Time

I

Phantasmal fears,
And the flap of the flame,
And the throb of the clock,
And a loosened slate,
And the blind night's drone,
Which tiredly the spectral pines intone!

II

And the blood in my ears
Strumming always the same,
And the gable-cock
With its fitful grate,
And myself, alone.

III

The twelfth hour nears
Hand-hid, as in shame;
I undo the lock,
And listen, and wait
For the Young Unknown.

IV

In the dark there careers –
As if Death astride came
To numb all with his knock –
A horse at mad rate
Over rut and stone.

V

No figure appears,
No call of my name,
No sound but 'Tic-toc'
Without check. Past the gate
It clatters – is gone.

VI

What rider it bears
There is none to proclaim;
And the Old Year has struck,
And, scarce animate,
The New makes moan.

VII

Maybe that 'More Tears! –
More Famine and Flame –
More Severance and Shock!'
Is the order from Fate
That the Rider speeds on
To pale Europe; and tiredly the pines intone.

1915–1916

Rudyard Kipling (1865–1936)

Rudyard Kipling was born in Bombay, spent some unhappy years at boarding school in Britain, and returned to India as a journalist in 1882. In his day he was immensely popular, but as the mood of the times changed, he became regarded as excessively patriotic and insulting in his portrayal of Indian people. His War poems are typical of so many writers' early sensations about the War – full of pride as well as worry, feelings of honour as well as grief.

Gethsemane
1914–18

The Garden called Gethsemane
   In Picardy it was,
And there the people came to see
   The English soldiers pass.
We used to pass — we used to pass
   Or halt, as it might be.
And ship our masks in case of gas
   Beyond Gethsemane.

The Garden called Gethsemane,
   It held a pretty lass,
But all the time she talked to me
   I prayed my cup might pass.
The officer sat on the chair,
   The men lay on the grass,
And all the time we halted there
   I prayed my cup might pass.

It didn't pass — it didn't pass —
   It didn't pass from me.
I drank it when we met the gas
   Beyond Gethsemane!

A Song in Storm
1914–18

Be well assured that on our side
  The abiding oceans fight,
Though headlong wind and heaping tide
  Make us their sport to-night.
By force of weather, not of war,
  In jeopardy we steer:
Then welcome Fate's discourtesy
  Whereby it shall appear
    How in all time of our distress,
    And our deliverance too,
    The game is more than the player of the game,
    And the ship is more than the crew!

Out of the mist into the mirk
  The glimmering combers roll.
Almost these mindless waters work
  As though they had a soul —
Almost as though they leagued to whelm
  Our flag beneath their green:
Then welcome Fate's discourtesy
  Whereby it shall be seen, etc.

Be well assured, though wave and wind
  Have mightier blows in store,
That we who keep the watch assigned
  Must stand to it the more;
And as our streaming bows rebuke
  Each billow's baulked career,
Sing, welcome Fate's discourtesy
  Whereby it is made clear, etc.

No matter though our decks be swept
  And mast and timber crack —
We can make good all loss except
  The loss of turning back.
So, 'twixt these Devils and our deep
  Let courteous trumpets sound,
To welcome Fate's discourtesy
  Whereby it will be found, etc.

Be well assured, though in our power
  Is nothing left to give
But chance and place to meet the hour,
  And leave to strive to live,
Till these dissolve our Order holds,
  Our Service binds us here.
Then welcome Fate's discourtesy
  Whereby it is made clear
    How in all time of our distress,
    As in our triumph too,
    The game is more than the player of the game,
    And the ship is more than the crew!

Mesopotamia
1917

They shall not return to us, the resolute, the young,
   The eager and whole-hearted whom we gave:
But the men who left them thriftily to die in their own
     dung,
   Shall they come with years and honour to the grave?

They shall not return to us, the strong men coldly slain
   In sight of help denied from day to day:
But the men who edged their agonies and chid them in
    their pain,
   Are they too strong and wise to put away?

Our dead shall not return to us while Day and Night
    divide —
   Never while the bars of sunset hold.
But the idle-minded overlings who quibbled while they
    died,
   Shall they thrust for high employments as of old?

Shall we only threaten and be angry for an hour?
   When the storm is ended shall we find
How softly but how swiftly they have sidled back to
    power
   By the favour and contrivance of their kind?

Even while they soothe us, while they promise large
    amends,
  Even while they make a show of fear,
Do they call upon their debtors, and take counsel with
    their friends,
  To confirm and re-establish each career?

Their lives cannot repay us — their death could not
    undo —
  The shame that they have laid upon our race.
But the slothfulness that wasted and the arrogance that
    slew,
Shall we leave it unabated in its place?

The Verdicts
(Jutland)

Not in the thick of the fight,
   Not in the press of the odds,
Do the heroes come to their height,
   Or we know the demi-gods.

That stands over till peace.
   We can only perceive
Men returned from the seas,
   Very grateful for leave.

They grant us sudden days
   Snatched from their business of war;
But we are too close to appraise
   What manner of men they are.

And, whether their names go down
   With age-kept victories,
Or whether they battle and drown
   Unreckoned, is hid from our eyes.

They are too near to be great,
   But our children shall understand
When and how our fate
   Was changed, and by whose hand.

Our children shall measure their worth.
   We are content to be blind . . .
But we know that we walk on a new born earth
   With the saviours of mankind.

A Death-bed

'This is the State above the Law.
    The State exists for the State alone.'
(*This is a gland at the back of the jaw,
    And an answering lump by the collar-bone.*)

Some die shouting in gas or fire;
    Some die silent, by shell and shot.
Some die desperate, caught on the wire;
    Some die suddenly. This will not.

'Regis suprema voluntas Lex'
    (*It will follow the regular course of – throats.*)
Some die pinned by the broken decks,
    Some die sobbing between the boats.

Some die eloquent, pressed to death
    By the sliding trench, as their friends can hear.
Some die wholly in half a breath.
    Some – give trouble for half a year.

'There is neither Evil nor Good in life
    Except as the needs of the State ordain.'
(*Since it is rather too late for the knife,
    All we can do is to mask the pain.*)

Some die saintly in faith and hope –
    One died thus in a prison yard –
Some die broken by rape or the rope;
    Some die easily. This dies hard.

'I will dash to pieces who bar my way.
    Woe to the traitor! Woe to the weak!'
(*Let him write what he wishes to say.
    It tires him out if he tries to speak.*)

Some die quietly. Some abound
    In loud self-pity. Others spread
Bad morale through the cots around . . .
    This is a type that is better dead.

'The war was forced on me by my foes.
    All that I sought was the right to live.'
(*Don't be afraid of a triple dose;
    The pain will neutralize half we give.*

*Here are the needles. See that he dies
    While the effects of the drug endure . . .
What is the question he asks with his eyes? –
    Yes, All-Highest, to God, be sure.*)

A Dead Statesman

I could not dig: I dared not rob:
Therefore I lied to please the mob.
Now all my lies are proved untrue
And I must face the men I slew.
What tale shall serve me here among
Mine angry and defrauded young?

Rupert Brooke (1887–1915)

Rupert Brooke won a scholarship to King's College, Cambridge, where he began to establish his reputation as a poet. In 1914 he joined the Royal Naval Volunteer Reserve and died on St George's Day (23 April) in 1915, en route to Gallipoli, from septicaemia caused by a mosquito bite.

Brooke's five 'War Sonnets' were received ecstatically at the time and became best-sellers. Modern taste sometimes finds their attitude to the War uncomfortable. They come too close to glorifying events, ignoring the horror of war and instead conveying a sickly mix of emotion and patriotism. But it is important to remember that they represent the mood of the period – a time when people at home, understandably, wanted uplifting, moving words about dark events across the sea.

Five Sonnets of 1914

I   Peace

Now, God be thanked Who has matched us with His
    hour,
  And caught our youth, and wakened us from
      sleeping,
With hand made sure, clear eye, and sharpened power,
  To turn, as swimmers into cleanness leaping,
Glad from a world grown old and cold and weary,
  Leave the sick hearts that honour could not move,
And half-men, and their dirty songs and dreary,
  And all the little emptiness of love!

Oh! we, who have known shame, we have found release
    there,
  Where there's no ill, no grief, but sleep has
    mending,
    Naught broken save this body, lost but breath;
Nothing to shake the laughing heart's long peace there
  But only agony, and that has ending;
    And the worst friend and enemy is but Death.

II *Safety*

Dear! of all happy in the hour, most blest
   He who has found our hid security,
Assured in the dark tides of the world that rest,
   And heard our word, 'Who is so safe as we?'
We have found safety with all things undying,
   The winds, and morning, tears of men and mirth,
The deep night, and birds singing, and clouds flying,
   And sleep, and freedom, and the autumnal earth.

We have built a house that is not for Time's throwing.
   We have gained a peace unshaken by pain for ever.
War knows no power. Safe shall be my going,
   Secretly armed against all death's endeavour;
Safe though all safety's lost; safe where men fall;
   And if these poor limbs die, safest of all.

III   The Dead

Blow out, you bugles, over the rich Dead!
  There's none of these so lonely and poor of old,
  But, dying, has made us rarer gifts than gold.
These laid the world away; poured out the red
Sweet wine of youth; gave up the years to be
  Of work and joy, and that unhoped serene,
  That men call age; and those who would have been,
Their sons, they gave, their immortality.
Blow, bugles, blow! They brought us, for our dearth,
  Holiness, lacked so long, and Love, and Pain.
Honour has come back, as a king, to earth,
  And paid his subjects with a royal wage;
And Nobleness walks in our ways again;
  And we have come into our heritage.

IV   The Dead

These hearts were woven of human joys and cares,
  Washed marvellously with sorrow, swift to mirth.
The years had given them kindness. Dawn was theirs,
  And sunset, and the colours of the earth.
These had seen movement, and heard music; known
  Slumber and waking; loved; gone proudly friended;
Felt the quick stir of wonder; sat alone;
  Touched flowers and furs and cheeks. All this is
    ended.

There are waters blown by changing winds to laughter
And lit by the rich skies, all day. And after,
   Frost, with a gesture, stays the waves that dance
And wandering loveliness. He leaves a white
   Unbroken glory, a gathered radiance,
A width, a shining peace, under the night.

V   *The Soldier*

If I should die, think only this of me:
   That there's some corner of a foreign field
That is for ever England. There shall be
   In that rich earth a richer dust concealed;
A dust whom England bore, shaped, made aware,
   Gave, once, her flowers to love, her ways to roam,
A body of England's, breathing English air,
   Washed by the rivers, blest by suns of home.

And think, this heart, all evil shed away,
   A pulse in the eternal mind, no less
      Gives somewhere back the thoughts by England
         given;
Her sights and sounds; dreams happy as her day;
   And laughter, learnt of friends; and gentleness,
      In hearts at peace, under an English heaven.

November–December 1914

Later voices

Siegfried Sassoon (1886–1967)

Although his parents separated when he was three, after which he saw little of his father, Sassoon had a comfortable childhood, hunting, playing cricket, and being educated at a public school. After Marlborough College he studied at Cambridge University. Whilst there he lived at home and wrote poetry.

When war loomed Sassoon enlisted as a trooper and then served as a fusilier on the Western Front, earning a Military Cross and the nickname 'Mad Jack' as a result of his reckless courage.

He went to war full of ideals and illusions. These were quickly shattered and fierce disillusionment runs through all of his poems. He frequently criticises the incompetence of those who conduct the War, and the lack of concern of those at home.

After the War he helped to establish the reputation of Wilfred Owen, editing a volume of his poetry. He also lent financial support to Robert Graves for publication of **Goodbye To All That**.

A Night Attack

The rank stench of those bodies haunts me still,
And I remember things I'd best forget.
For now we've marched to a green, trenchless land
Twelve miles from battering guns: along the grass
Brown lines of tents are hives for snoring men;
Wide, radiant water sways the floating sky
Below dark, shivering trees. And living-clean
Comes back with thoughts of home and hours of sleep.

To-night I smell the battle; miles away
Gun-thunder leaps and thuds along the ridge;
The spouting shells dig pits in fields of death,
And wounded men are moaning in the woods.
If any friend be there whom I have loved,
God speed him safe to England with a gash.

It's sundown in the camp; some youngster laughs,
Lifting his mug and drinking health to all
Who come unscathed from that unpitying waste.
(Terror and ruin lurk behind his gaze.)
Another sits with tranquil, musing face,
Puffing his pipe and dreaming of the girl
Whose last scrawled letter lies upon his knee.
The sunlight falls, low-ruddy from the west,
Upon their heads; last week they might have died;
And now they stretch their limbs in tired content.

One says 'The bloody Bosche has got the knock;
And soon they'll crumple up and chuck their games.
We've got the beggars on the run at last!'

Then I remembered someone that I'd seen
Dead in a squalid, miserable ditch,
Heedless of toiling feet that trod him down.
He was a Prussian with a decent face,
Young, fresh, and pleasant, so I dare to say.
No doubt he loathed the war and longed for peace,
And cursed our souls because we'd killed his friends.

One night he yawned along a half-dug trench
Midnight; and then the British guns began
With heavy shrapnel bursting low, and 'hows'
Whistling to cut the wire with blinding din.
  He didn't move; the digging still went on;
Men stooped and shovelled; someone gave a grunt,
And moaned and died with agony in the sludge.
Then the long hiss of shells lifted and stopped.

He stared into the gloom; a rocket curved,
And rifles rattled angrily on the left
Down by the wood, and there was noise of bombs.
  Then the damned English loomed in scrambling haste
Out of the dark and struggled through the wire,
And there were shouts and curses; someone screamed
And men began to blunder down the trench
Without their rifles. It was time to go:
He grabbed his coat; stood up, gulping some bread;
Then clutched his head and fell.
                        I found him there
In the gray morning when the place was held.
His face was in the mud; one arm flung out
As when he crumpled up; his sturdy legs
Were beneath his trunk, heels to the sky.

July 1916

Twelve Months After

Hullo! here's my platoon, the lot I had last year.
'The war'll be over soon.'
                    'What 'opes?'
                              'No bloody fear!'
Then, 'Number Seven, 'shun! All present and correct.'
They're standing in the sun, impassive and erect.
Young Gibson with his grin; and Morgan, tired and white;
Jordan, who's out to win a D.C.M. some night;
And Hughes that's keen on wiring; and Davies ('79),
Who always must be firing at the Bosche front line.

                    .   .   .

'Old soldiers never die; they simply fide a-why!'
That's what they used to sing along the roads last spring;
That's what they used to say before the push began;
That's where they are to-day, knocked over to a man.

Craiglockhart, 1917

Does It Matter?

Does it matter? — losing your legs? . . .
For people will always be kind,
And you need not show that you mind
When the others come in after hunting
To gobble their muffins and eggs.

27

Does it matter? — losing your sight? . . .
There's such splendid work for the blind;
And people will always be kind,
As you sit on the terrace remembering
And turning your face to the light.

Do they matter? — those dreams from the pit? . . .
You can drink and forget and be glad,
And people won't say that you're mad;
For they'll know that you've fought for your country
And no one will worry a bit.

Craiglockhart 1917

The General

'Good-morning, good-morning!' the General said
When we met him last week on our way to the line.
Now the soldiers he smiled at are most of 'em dead,
And we're cursing his staff for incompetent swine.
'He's a cheery old card,' grunted Harry to Jack
As they slogged up to Arras with rifle and pack.

.　　.　　.

But he did for them both by his plan of attack.

Denmark Hill Hospital, April 1917

The Dug-Out

Why do you lie with your legs ungainly huddled,
And one arm bent across your sullen, cold,
Exhausted face? It hurts my heart to watch you,
Deep-shadow'd from the candle's guttering gold;
And you wonder why I shake you by the shoulder;
Drowsy, you mumble and sigh and turn your head . . .
You are too young to fall asleep for ever;
And when you sleep you remind me of the dead.

St Venant, July 1918

Aftermath

Have you forgotten yet? . . .
For the world's events have rumbled on since those
    gagged days,
Like traffic checked while at the crossing of city-ways:
And the haunted gap in your mind has filled with
    thoughts that flow
Like clouds in the lit heaven of life; and you're a man
    reprieved to go,
Taking your peaceful share of Time, with joy to spare.
But the past is just the same — and War's a bloody game . . .
Have you forgotten yet? . . .
Look down, and swear by the slain of the War that you'll never
    forget.

29

Do you remember the dark months you held the sector
    at Mametz —
The nights you watched and wired and dug and piled
    sandbags on parapets?
Do you remember the rats; and the stench
Of corpses rotting in front of the front-line trench—
And dawn coming, dirty-white, and chill with a hopeless
    rain?
Do you ever stop and ask, 'Is it all going to happen
    again?'

Do you remember that hour of din before the attack—
And the anger, the blind compassion that seized and
    shook you

As you peered at the doomed and haggard faces of your
    men?
Do you remember the stretcher-cases lurching back
With dying eyes and lolling heads — those ashen-grey
Masks of the lads who once were keen and kind and
    gay?

Have you forgotten yet? . . .
Look up, and swear by the green of the spring that you'll never
    forget.

                                   March 1919

Isaac Rosenberg (1890–1918)

The eldest son of Lithuanian Jewish immigrants, Rosenberg was born in Bristol but moved to London when he was seven. He was brought up in one room with his six brothers and sisters and left school at the age of fourteen to help supplement the family income by becoming an apprentice engraver. He disliked the work and was rescued by patrons in 1911 who recognised his artistic talent and funded his progress through the Slade School of Art.

He was in Cape Town, South Africa, when war broke out, and joined up for financial rather than patriotic reasons. He hated the army and had hoped to join a medical unit, rather than be involved in killing people. He was too short and found himself in the King's Own Royal Lancasters in June 1916.

He tried to escape the horrors of war through writing and his best known poem – 'Break of Day in the Trenches' – was published in December 1916.

Rosenberg was killed during night patrol near Arras, France, as April Fool's Day 1918 dawned. His body was never found. His reputation as a poet has grown during the century and he is now generally regarded as one of the finest of the War poets.

Break of Day in the Trenches

The darkness crumbles away –
It is the same old druid Time as ever.
Only a live thing leaps my hand
A queer sardonic rat –
As I pulled the parapet's poppy
To stick behind my ear.
Droll rat, they would shoot you if they knew
Your cosmopolitan sympathies.
Now you have touched this English hand
You will do the same to a German –
Soon, no doubt, if it be your pleasure
To cross the sleeping green between.
It seems you inwardly grin as you pass
Strong eyes, fine limbs, haughty athletes
Less chanced than you for life,
Bonds to the whims of murder,
Sprawled in the bowels of the earth,
The torn fields of France.
What do you see in our eyes
At the shrieking iron and flame
Hurled through still heavens?
What quaver – what heart aghast?
Poppies whose roots are in man's veins
Drop, and are ever dropping;
But mine in my ear is safe,
Just a little white with the dust.

1917

Louse Hunting

Nudes – stark and glistening,
Yelling in lurid glee. Grinning faces
And raging limbs
Whirl over the floor one fire.
For a shirt verminously busy
Yon soldier tore from his throat, with oaths
Godhead might shrink at, but not the lice.
And soon the shirt was aflare
Over the candle he'd lit while we lay.

Then we all sprang up and stript
To hunt the verminous brood.
Soon like a demons' pantomime
The place was raging.
See the silhouettes agape,
See the gibbering shadows
Mixed with the battled arms on the wall.
See gargantuan hooked fingers
Pluck in supreme flesh
To smutch supreme littleness.
See the merry limbs in hot Highland fling
Because some wizard vermin
Charmed from the quiet this revel
When our ears were half lulled
By the dark music
Blown from Sleep's trumpet.

1917

Returning, We Hear the Larks

Sombre the night is.
And though we have our lives, we know
What sinister threat lurks there.

Dragging these anguished limbs, we only know
This poison-blasted track opens on our camp –
On a little safe sleep.

But hark! joy – joy – strange joy.
Lo! heights of night ringing with unseen larks.
Music showering on our upturned list'ning faces.

Death could drop from the dark
As easily as song –
But song only dropped,
Like a blind man's dreams on the sand
By dangerous tides,
Like a girl's dark hair for she dreams no ruin lies there,
Or her kisses where a serpent hides.

1917

The Dying Soldier

'Here are houses,' he moaned.
'I could reach but my brain swims.'
Then they thundered and flashed
And shook the earth to its rims.

'They are gunpits,' he gasped,
'Our men are at the guns.
Water – water – O water
For one of England's dying sons.'

'We cannot give you water
Were all England in your breath.'
'Water – water – O water'
He moaned and swooned to death.

1917

Dead Man's Dump

The plunging limbers over the shattered track
Racketed with their rusty freight,
Stuck out like many crowns of thorns,
And the rusty stakes like sceptres old
To stay the flood of brutish men
Upon our brothers dear.

The wheels lurched over sprawled dead
But pained them not, though their bones crunched,
Their shut mouths made no moan.
They lie there huddled, friend and foeman,
Man born of man, and born of woman,
And shells go crying over them
From night till night and now.

Earth has waited for them,
All the time of their growth
Fretting for their decay:
Now she has them at last!
In the strength of their strength
Suspended – stopped and held.

What fierce imaginings their dark souls lit?
Earth! have they gone into you!
Somewhere they must have gone,
And flung on your hard back
Is their soul's sack
Emptied of God-ancestralled essences.
Who hurled them out? Who hurled?

None saw their spirits' shadow shake the grass,
Or stood aside for the half used life to pass
Out of those doomed nostrils and the doomed mouth,
When the swift iron burning bee
Drained the wild honey of their youth.

What of us who, flung on the shrieking pyre,
Walk, our usual thoughts untouched,
Our lucky limbs as on ichor fed,
Immortal seeming ever?
Perhaps when the flames beat loud on us,
A fear may choke in our veins
And the startled blood may stop.

The air is loud with death,
The dark air spurts with fire,
The explosions ceaseless are.
Timelessly now, some minutes past,
These dead strode time with vigorous life,
Till the shrapnel called 'An end!'
But not to all. In bleeding pangs
Some borne on stretchers dreamed of home,
Dear things, war-blotted from their hearts.

Maniac Earth! howling and flying, your bowel
Seared by the jagged fire, the iron love,
The impetuous storm of savage love.
Dark Earth! dark Heavens! swinging in chemic smoke,
What dead are born when you kiss each soundless soul
With lightning and thunder from your mined heart,
Which man's self dug, and his blind fingers loosed?

A man's brains splattered on
A stretcher-bearer's face;
His shook shoulders slipped their load,

But when they bent to look again
The drowning soul was sunk too deep
For human tenderness.

They left this dead with the older dead,
Stretched at the cross roads.

Burnt black by strange decay
Their sinister faces lie,
The lid over each eye,
The grass and coloured clay
More motion have than they,
Joined to the great sunk silences.

Here is one not long dead;
His dark hearing caught our far wheels,
And the choked soul stretched weak hands
To reach the living word the far wheels said,
The blood-dazed intelligence beating for light,
Crying through the suspense of the far torturing wheels
Swift for the end to break
Or the wheels to break,
Cried as the tide of the world broke over his sight.
Will they come? Will they ever come?
Even as the mixed hoofs of the mules,
The quivering-bellied mules,
And the rushing wheels all mixed
With his tortured upturned sight.
So we crashed round the bend,
We heard his weak scream,
We heard his very last sound,
And our wheels grazed his dead face.

1918

Wilfred Owen (1893–1918)

The oldest son of a railway clerk, Wilfred Owen was keen to do well at school in Birkenhead, near Liverpool. He read the works of Shakespeare and the Romantic poets (especially Keats) and modelled his own poetry on their work. In 1913 he began to teach English in southern France, and was there when war was declared in 1914.

Returning to England, Owen joined the Artists' Rifles and became second lieutenant with the Manchester Regiment. He went on active service in the summer of 1916 and was deeply affected by the horrors of trench warfare. He wrote intensely about the individual sufferings of the soldiers around him.

He met Siegfried Sassoon in hospital in Edinburgh in 1917, whilst recovering from shell-shock. Sassoon had an important impact on Owen's poetry, making him more experimental in his technique. He returned to France in September 1918 and was killed on 4 November, just a week before the end of the War.

Anthem for Doomed Youth

What passing-bells for these who die as cattle?
 – Only the monstrous anger of the guns.
 Only the stuttering rifles' rapid rattle
Can patter out their hasty orisons.
No mockeries now for them; no prayers nor bells;
 Nor any voice of mourning save the choirs, –
The shrill, demented choirs of wailing shells;
 And bugles calling for them from sad shires.

What candles may be held to speed them all?
 Not in the hands of boys but in their eyes
Shall shine the holy glimmers of goodbyes.
 The pallor of girls' brows shall be their pall;
Their flowers the tenderness of patient minds,
And each slow dusk a drawing-down of blinds.

1917

Strange Meeting

It seemed that out of battle I escaped
Down some profound dull tunnel, long since scooped
Through granites which titanic wars had groined.

Yet also there encumbered sleepers groaned,
Too fast in thought or death to be bestirred.
Then, as I probed them, one sprang up, and stared
With piteous recognition in fixed eyes,
Lifting distressful hands, as if to bless.
And by his smile, I knew that sullen hall, –
By his dead smile I knew we stood in Hell.

With a thousand pains that vision's face was grained;
Yet no blood reached there from the upper ground,
And no guns thumped, or down the flues made moan.
'Strange friend,' I said, 'here is no cause to mourn.'
'None,' said that other, 'save the undone years,
The hopelessness. Whatever hope is yours,
Was my life also; I went hunting wild
After the wildest beauty in the world,
Which lies not calm in eyes, or braided hair,
But mocks the steady running of the hour,
And if it grieves, grieves richlier than here.
For by my glee might many men have laughed,
And of my weeping something had been left,
Which must die now. I mean the truth untold,
The pity of war, the pity war distilled.
Now men will go content with what we spoiled,
Or, discontent, boil bloody, and be spilled.
They will be swift with swiftness of the tigress.

None will break ranks, though nations trek from
  progress.
Courage was mine, and I had mystery,
Wisdom was mine, and I had mastery:
To miss the march of this retreating world
Into vain citadels that are not walled.
Then, when much blood had clogged their
  chariot-wheels,
I would go up and wash them from sweet wells.
Even with truths that lie too deep for taint.
I would have poured my spirit without stint
But not through wounds; not on the cess of war.
Foreheads of men have bled where no wounds were.

'I am the enemy you killed, my friend.
I knew you in this dark: for so you frowned
Yesterday through me as you jabbed and killed.
I parried; but my hands were loath and cold.
Let us sleep now . . .'

1918

Dulce et Decorum Est

Bent double, like old beggars under sacks,
Knock-kneed, coughing like hags, we cursed through sludge,
Till on the haunting flares we turned our backs
And towards our distant rest began to trudge.
Men marched asleep. Many had lost their boots
But limped on, blood-shod. All went lame; all blind;
Drunk with fatigue, deaf even to the hoots
Of tired, outstripped Five-Nines that dropped behind.

Gas! GAS! Quick, boys! – An ecstasy of fumbling,
Fitting the clumsy helmets just in time;
But someone still was yelling out and stumbling,
And flound'ring like a man in fire or lime . . .
Dim, through the misty panes and thick green light,
As under a green sea, I saw him drowning.

In all my dreams, before my helpless sight,
He plunges at me, guttering, choking, drowning.

If in some smothering dreams you too could pace
Behind the wagon that we flung him in,
And watch the white eyes writhing in his face,
His hanging face, like a devil's sick of sin;
If you could hear, at every jolt, the blood
Come gargling from the froth-corrupted lungs,
Obscene as cancer, bitter as the cud
Of vile, incurable sores on innocent tongues, –
My friend, you would not tell with such high zest
To children ardent for some desperate glory,
The old Lie: Dulce et decorum est
Pro patria mori.

1917

Futility

Move him into the sun –
Gently its touch awoke him once,
At home, whispering of fields half-sown.
Always it woke him, even in France,
Until this morning and this snow.
If anything might rouse him now
The kind old sun will know.

Think how it wakes the seeds –
Woke once the clays of a cold star.
Are limbs, so dear achieved, are sides
Full-nerved, still warm, too hard to stir?
 Was it for this the clay grew tall?
– O what made fatuous sunbeams toil
To break earth's sleep at all?

1918

Disabled

He sat in a wheeled chair, waiting for dark,
And shivered in his ghastly suit of grey,
Legless, sewn short at elbow. Through the park
Voices of boys rang saddening like a hymn,
Voices of play and pleasure after day,
Till gathering sleep had mothered them from him.

.　　.　　.

About this time Town used to swing so gay
When glow-lamps budded in the light blue trees,
And girls glanced lovelier as the air grew dim, –
In the old times, before he threw away his knees.
Now he will never feel again how slim
Girls' waists are, or how warm their subtle hands.
All of them touch him like some queer disease.

.　　.　　.

There was an artist silly for his face,
For it was younger than his youth, last year.
Now, he is old; his back will never brace;
He's lost his colour very far from here,
Poured it down shell-holes till the veins ran dry,
And half his lifetime lapsed in the hot race
And leap of purple spurted from his thigh.

.　　.　　.

One time he liked a blood-smear down his leg,
After the matches, carried shoulder-high.
It was after football, when he'd drunk a peg,
He thought he'd better join. – He wonders why.
Someone had said he'd look a god in kilts,
That's why; and maybe, too, to please his Meg.
Aye, that was it, to please the giddy jilts
He asked to join. He didn't have to beg;
Smiling they wrote his lie: aged nineteen years.

.   .   .

Germans he scarcely thought of; all their guilt,
And Austria's, did not move him. And no fears
Of Fear came yet. He thought of jewelled hilts
For daggers in plaid socks; of smart salutes;
And care of arms; and leave; and pay arrears;
Esprit de corps; and hints for young recruits.
And soon, he was drafted out with drums and cheers.

.   .   .

Some cheered him home, but not as crowds cheer Goal.
Only a solemn man who brought his fruits
Thanked him; and then enquired about his soul.

.   .   .

Now, he will spend a few sick years in institutes,
And do what things the rules consider wise,
And take whatever pity they may dole.
Tonight he noticed how the women's eyes
Passed from him to the strong men that were whole.
How cold and late it is! Why don't they come
And put him into bed? Why don't they come?

1917

Exposure

Our brains ache, in the merciless iced east winds that
    knive us . . .
Wearied we keep awake because the night is silent . . .
Low, drooping flares confuse our memory of the
    salient . . .
Worried by silence, sentries whisper, curious, nervous,
       But nothing happens.

Watching, we hear the mad gusts tugging on the wire,
Like twitching agonies of men among its brambles.
Northward, incessantly, the flickering gunnery rumbles,
Far off, like a dull rumour of some other war.
       What are we doing here?

The poignant misery of dawn begins to grow . . .
We only know war lasts, rain soaks, and clouds sag
    stormy.
Dawn massing in the east her melancholy army
Attacks once more in ranks on shivering ranks of grey,
       But nothing happens.

Sudden successive flights of bullets streak the silence.
Less deathly than the air that shudders black with snow,
With sidelong flowing flakes that flock, pause, and
    renew;
We watch them wandering up and down the wind's
    nonchalance,
       But nothing happens.

Pale flakes with fingering stealth come feeling for our
    faces –
We cringe in holes, back on forgotten dreams, and
    stare, snow-dazed,
Deep into grassier ditches. So we drowse, sun-dozed,
Littered with blossoms trickling where the blackbird
    fusses,
       – Is it that we are dying?

Slowly our ghosts drag home: glimpsing the sunk fires,
    glozed
With crusted dark-red jewels; crickets jingle there;
For hours the innocent mice rejoice: the house is theirs;
Shutters and doors, all closed: on us the doors are
    closed, –
       We turn back to our dying.

Since we believe not otherwise can kind fires burn;
Nor ever suns smile true on child, or field, or fruit.
For God's invincible spring our love is made afraid;
Therefore, not loath, we lie out here; therefore were
    born,
       For love of God seems dying.

Tonight, this frost will fasten on this mud and us,
Shrivelling many hands, puckering foreheads crisp.
The burying-party, picks and shovels in shaking grasp,
Pause over half-known faces. All their eyes are ice,
       But nothing happens.

1918

The Sentry

We'd found an old Boche dug-out, and he knew,
And gave us hell, for shell on frantic shell
Hammered on top, but never quite burst through.
Rain, guttering down in waterfalls of slime,
Kept slush waist high that, rising hour by hour,
Choked up the steps too thick with clay to climb.
What murk of air remained stank old, and sour
With fumes of whizz-bangs, and the smell of men
Who'd lived there years, and left their curse in the den,
If not their corpses . . .
           There we herded from the blast
Of whizz-bangs, but one found our door at last.
Buffeting eyes and breath, snuffing the candles,
And thud! flump! thud! down the steep steps came
   thumping
And sploshing in the flood, deluging muck –
The sentry's body; then his rifle, handles
Of old Boche bombs, and mud in ruck on ruck.
We dredged him up, for killed, until he whined
'O sir, my eyes – I'm blind – I'm blind, I'm blind!'
Coaxing, I held a flame against his lids
And said if he could see the least blurred light
He was not blind; in time he'd get all right.
'I can't,' he sobbed. Eyeballs, huge-bulged like squids',
Watch my dreams still; but I forgot him there
In posting next for duty, and sending a scout
To beg a stretcher somewhere, and floundering about
To other posts under the shrieking air.

49

Those other wretches, how they bled and spewed,
And one who would have drowned himself for good, –
I try not to remember these things now.
Let dread hark back for one word only: how
Half-listening to that sentry's moans and jumps,
And the wild chattering of his broken teeth,
Renewed most horribly whenever crumps
Pummelled the roof and slogged the air beneath –
Through the dense din, I say, we heard him shout
'I see your lights!' But ours had long died out.

1918

Edmund Blunden (1896–1974)

Edmund Blunden enlisted in the Royal Sussex Regiment in 1915, describing himself as 'a harmless young shepherd in a soldier's coat'. His poetry, which he had begun to write at Oxford, showed a genuine understanding of the countryside – not simply the pastoral clichés which had become fashionable in much poetry of the period.

He won the Military Cross as a second lieutenant, before being sent home to England in the spring of 1918 after having been gassed. He commented in 1973: 'My experiences in the First World War have haunted me all my life, and for many days I have, it seemed, lived in that world rather than this.'

After the War, Blunden became a scholar at Tokyo University and then Oxford. He published a huge quantity of poetry, reviews, articles, and editions of other writers' work – notably Wilfred Owen and the neglected country poet, John Clare.

His own poetry often contrasts the gentleness of the countryside with the human violence which destroys it.

The Zonnebeke Road

Morning, if this late withered light can claim
Some kindred with that merry flame
Which the young day was wont to fling through space!
Agony stares from each grey face.
And yet the day is come; stand down! stand down!
Your hands unclasp from rifles while you can;
The frost has pierced them to the bended bone?
Why, see old Stevens there, that iron man,
Melting the ice to shave his grotesque chin!
Go ask him, shall we win?
I never liked this bay, some foolish fear
Caught me the first time that I came in here;
That dugout fallen in awakes, perhaps,
Some formless haunting of some corpse's chaps.
True, and wherever we have held the line,
There were such corners, seeming-saturnine
For no good cause.
                    Now where Haymarket starts,
That is no place for soldiers with weak hearts;
The minenwerfers have it to the inch.
Look, how the snow-dust whisks along the road
Piteous and silly; the stones themselves must flinch
In this east wind; the low sky like a load
Hangs over, a dead-weight. But what a pain
Must gnaw where its clay cheek
Crushes the shell-chopped trees that fang the plain –
The ice-bound throat gulps out a gargoyle shriek.
That wretched wire before the village line
Rattles like rusty brambles or dead bine,
And there the daylight oozes into dun;

Black pillars, those are trees where roadways run.
Even Ypres now would warm our souls; fond fool,
Our tour's but one night old, seven more to cool!
O screaming dumbness, O dull crashing death,
Shreds of dead grass and willows, homes and men,
Watch as you will, men clench their chattering teeth
And freeze you back with that one hope, disdain.

Third Ypres

Triumph! How strange, how strong had triumph come
On weary hate of foul and endless war
When from its grey gravecloths awoke anew
The summer day. Among the tumbled wreck
Of fascined lines and mounds the light was pecring,
Half-smiling upon us, and our newfound pride;
The terror of the waiting night outlived,
The time too crowded for the heart to count
All the sharp cost in friends killed on the assault.
No hook of all the octopus had held us,
Here stood we trampling down the ancient tyrant.
So shouting dug we among the monstrous pits.
Amazing quiet fell upon the waste,
Quiet intolerable to those who felt
The hurrying batteries beyond the masking hills
For their new parley setting themselves in array
In crafty forms unmapped.
                                        No, these, smiled Faith,
Are dumb for the reason of their overthrow.
They move not back, they lie among the crews
Twisted and choked, they'll never speak again.
Only the copse where once might stand a shrine
Still clacked and suddenly hissed its bullets by.
The War would end, the Line was on the move,
And at a bound the impassable was passed.
We lay and waited with extravagant joy.

Now dulls the day and chills; comes there no word
From those who swept through our new lines to flood
The lines beyond? but little comes, and so

Sure as a runner time himself's accosted.
And the slow moments shake their heavy heads,
And croak, 'They're done, they'll none of them get
    through.
They're done, they've all died on the entanglements,
The wire stood up like an unplashed hedge and
    thorned
With giant spikes – and there they've paid the bill.'
Then comes the black assurance, then the sky's
Mute misery lapses into trickling rain,
That wreathes and swims and soon shuts in our world,
And those distorted guns, that lay past use,
Why – miracles not over! – all a-firing!
The rain's no cloak from their sharp eyes. And you,
Poor signaller, you I passed by this emplacement,
You whom I warned, poor daredevil, waving your flags,
Among this screeching I pass you again and shudder
At the lean green flies upon the red flesh madding.
Runner, stand by a second. Your message. – He's gone,
Falls on a knee, and his right hand uplifted
Claws his last message from his ghostly enemy,
Turns stone-like. Well I liked him, that young runner,
But there's no time for that. O now for the word
To order us flash from these drowning roaring traps
And even hurl upon that snarling wire?
Why are our guns so impotent?
                              The grey rain,
Steady as the sand in an hourglass on this day,
Where through the window the red lilac looks,
And all's so still, the chair's odd click is noise –
The rain is all heaven's answer, and with hearts
Past reckoning we are carried into night
And even sleep is nodding here and there.

The second night steals through the shrouding rain.
We in our numb thought crouching long have lost
The mockery triumph, and in every runner
Have urged the mind's eye see the triumph to come
The sweet relief, the straggling out of hell
Into whatever burrows may be given
For life's recall. Then the fierce destiny speaks.
This was the calm, we shall look back for this.
The hour is come; come, move to the relief!
Dizzy we pass the mule-strewn track where once
The ploughman whistled as he loosed his team;
And where he turned home-hungry on the road,
The leaning pollard marks us hungrier turning.
We crawl to save the remnant who have torn
Back from the tentacled wire, those whom no shell
Has charred into black carcasses – Relief!
They grate their teeth until we take their room,
And through the churn of moonless night and mud
And flaming burst and sour gas we are huddled
Into the ditches where they bawl sense awake,
And in a frenzy that none could reason calm
(Whimpering some, and calling on the dead),
They turn away: as in a dream they find
Strength in their feet to bear back that strange whim
Their body.
        At the noon of the dreadful day
Our trench and death's is on a sudden stormed
With huge and shattering salvoes, the clay dances
In founts of clods around the concrete sties,
Where still the brain devises some last armour
To live out the poor limbs.
              This wrath's oncoming
Found four of us together in a pillbox,

Skirting the abyss of madness with light phrases,
White and blinking, in false smiles grimacing.
The demon grins to see the game, a moment
Passes, and – still the drum-tap dongs my brain
To a whirring void – through the great breach above me
The light comes in with icy shock and the rain
Horribly drips. Doctor, talk talk! if dead
Or stunned I know not; the stinking powdered
   concrete,
The lyddite turns me sick – my hair's all full
Of this smashed concrete. O, I'll drag you, friends,
Out of the sepulchre into the light of day,
For this is day, the pure and sacred day.
And while I squeak and gibber over you,
Look, from the wreck a score of field-mice nimble,
And tame and curious look about them; (these
Calmed me, on these depended my salvation).
There comes my sergeant, and by all the powers
The wire is holding to the right battalion,
And I can speak – but I myself first spoken
Hear a known voice now measured even to madness
Call me by name.

        'For God's sake send and help us,
Here in a gunpit, all headquarters done for,
Forty or more, the nine-inch came right through,
All splashed with arms and legs, and I myself
The only one not killed nor even wounded.
You'll send – God bless you!' The more monstrous fate
Shadows our own, the mind swoons doubly burdened,
Taught how for miles our anguish groans and bleeds,
A whole sweet countryside amuck with murder;
Each moment puffed into a year with death
Still wept the rain, roared guns,

Still swooped into the swamps of flesh and blood,
All to the drabness of uncreation sunk,
And all thought dwindled to a moan, Relieve!
But who with what command can now relieve
The dead men from that chaos, or my soul?

The Ancre at Hamel: Afterwards

Where tongues were loud and hearts were light
    I heard the Ancre flow;
Waking oft at the mid of night
    I heard the Ancre flow.

I heard it crying, that sad rill,
    Below the painful ridge
By the burnt unraftered mill
    And the relic of a bridge.

And could this sighing river seem
    To call me far away,
And its pale word dismiss as dream
    The voices of to-day?
The voices in the bright room chilled
    And that mourned on alone;
The silence of the full moon filled
    With that brook's troubling tone.

The struggling Ancre had no part
    In these new hours of mine,
And yet its stream ran through my heart;
    I heard it grieve and pine,
As if its rainy tortured blood
    Had swirled into my own,
When by its battered bank I stood
    And shared its wounded moan.

1916 Seen from 1921

Tired with dull grief, grown old before my day,
I sit in solitude and only hear
Long silent laughters, murmurings of dismay,
The lost intensities of hope and fear;
In those old marshes yet the rifles lie,
On the thin breastwork flutter the grey rags,
The very books I read are there – and I
Dead as the men I loved, wait while life drags

Its wounded length from those sad streets of war
Into green places here, that were my own;
But now what once was mine is mine no more,
I seek such neighbours here and I find none.
With such strong gentleness and tireless will
Those ruined houses seared themselves in me,
Passionate I look for their dumb story still,
And the charred stub outspeaks the living tree.

I rise up at the singing of a bird
And scarcely knowing slink along the lane,
I dare not give a soul a look or word
Where all have homes and none's at home in vain:
Deep red the rose burned in the grim redoubt,
The self-sown wheat around was like a flood,
In the hot path the lizard lolled time out,
The saints in broken shrines were bright as blood.

Sweet Mary's shrine between the sycamores!
There we would go, my friends of friends and I,
And snatch long moments from the grudging wars,
Whose dark made light intense to see them by.
Shrewd bit the morning fog, the whining shots
Spun from the wrangling wire; then in warm swoon
The sun hushed all but the cool orchard plots,
We crept in the tall grass and slept till noon.

Poems by women

The women writers are chiefly writing from home, attempting to come to terms with the horrors at the front. They were not enlisted to fight, but sometimes served as nurses and ambulance drivers. Their views counterbalance the mostly male agony of the front lines – the grim vision of the First World War which generations have become so familiar with. They add their own important voices of suffering and anxiety, patriotism and shame, hope and despair.

Edna St Vincent Millay (1892–1950) was an American poet who in the 1920s established herself as a controversial, often rebellious voice.

Vera Brittain (1896–1970) was a writer and pacifist, best known for her autobiography, *Testament of Youth*, about her childhood and War experiences. She left Oxford University early to serve as a voluntary nurse. Her poem here is dedicated to her fiancé.

May Wedderburn Cannan (1893–1973) was a poet and novelist. She served in the Voluntary Aid Detachment and then in the Intelligence Service during the War.

Margaret Postgate Cole (1893–1980) worked briefly as a classics teacher before taking up political work with the Fabian Society. She wrote several books – including many detective novels.

Eleanor Farjeon (1881–1965) was born in London and became well known for her children's stories. Her work is commemorated in a Farjeon Award for outstanding work in children's literature.

Margaret Sackville (1881–1963) was mainly a poet, although she wrote some books for children.

It was not possible to find biographical information on **Mary H. J. Henderson**.

Edna St Vincent Millay

Conscientious Objector

I shall die, but that is all that I shall do for Death.

I hear him leading his horse out of the stall; I hear the
    clatter on the barn-floor.
He is in haste; he has business in Cuba, business in the
    Balkans, many calls to make this morning.
But I will not hold the bridle while he cinches the girth.
And he may mount by himself: I will not give him a leg up.

Though he flick my shoulders with his whip, I will not
    tell him which way the fox ran.
With his hoof on my breast, I will not tell him where the
    black boy hides in the swamp.
I shall die, but that is all that I shall do for Death; I am
    not on his pay-roll.

I will not tell him the whereabouts of my friends nor of
    my enemies either.
Though he promise me much, I will not map him the
    route to any man's door.

Am I a spy in the land of the living, that I should deliver
    men to Death?
Brother, the password and the plans of our city are safe
    with me; never through me
Shall you be overcome.

Vera Brittain

Perhaps—
(To R.A.L. Died of Wounds in France, December 23rd, 1915)

Perhaps some day the sun will shine again,
　　And I shall see that still the skies are blue,
And feel once more I do not live in vain,
　　Although bereft of You.

Perhaps the golden meadows at my feet
　　Will make the sunny hours of Spring seem gay,
And I shall find the white May blossoms sweet,
　　Though You have passed away.

Perhaps the summer woods will shimmer bright,
　　And crimson roses once again be fair,
And autumn harvest fields a rich delight,
　　Although You are not there.

Perhaps some day I shall not shrink in pain
　　To see the passing of the dying year,
And listen to the Christmas songs again,
　　Although You cannot hear.

But, though kind Time may many joys renew,
　　There is one greatest joy I shall not know
Again, because my heart for loss of You
　　Was broken, long ago.

1st London General Hospital, February 1916

May Wedderburn Cannan

Lamplight

We planned to shake the world together, you and I
Being young, and very wise;
Now in the light of the green shaded lamp
Almost I see your eyes
Light with the old gay laughter; you and I
Dreamed greatly of an Empire in those days,
Setting our feet upon laborious ways,
And all you asked of fame
Was crossed swords in the Army List,
My Dear, against your name.

We planned a great Empire together, you and I,
Bound only by the sea;
Now in the quiet of a chill Winter's night
Your voice comes hushed to me
Full of forgotten memories: you and I
Dreamed great dreams of our future in those days,
Setting our feet on undiscovered ways,
And all I asked of fame
A scarlet cross on my breast, my Dear,
For the swords by your name.

We shall never shake the world together, you and I,
For you gave your life away;
And I think my heart was broken by the war,
Since on a summer day
You took the road we never spoke of: you and I
Dreamed greatly of an Empire in those days;
You set your feet upon the Western ways
And have no need of fame –
There's a scarlet cross on my breast, my Dear,
And a torn cross with your name.

December 1916

Margaret Postgate Cole

The Falling Leaves

Today, as I rode by,
I saw the brown leaves dropping from their tree
In a still afternoon,
When no wind whirled them whistling to the sky,
But thickly, silently,
They fell, like snowflakes wiping out the noon;
And wandered slowly thence
For thinking of a gallant multitude
Which now all withering lay,
Slain by no wind of age or pestilence,
But in their beauty strewed
Like snowflakes falling on the Flemish clay.

November 1915

Eleanor Farjeon

Easter Monday
(In Memoriam E.T.)

In the last letter that I had from France
You thanked me for the silver Easter egg
Which I had hidden in the box of apples
You liked to munch beyond all other fruit.
You found the egg the Monday before Easter,
And said, 'I will praise Easter Monday now –
It was such a lovely morning.' Then you spoke
Of the coming battle and said, 'This is the eve.
Good-bye. And may I have a letter soon.'

That Easter Monday was a day for praise,
It was such a lovely morning. In our garden
We sowed our earliest seeds, and in the orchard
The apple-bud was ripe. It was the eve.
There are three letters that you will not get.

9 April 1917

Mary H. J. Henderson

An Incident

He was just a boy, as I could see,
For he sat in the tent there close by me.
I held the lamp with its flickering light,
And felt the hot tears blur my sight
As the doctor took the blood-stained bands
From both his brave, shell-shattered hands –
His boy hands, wounded more pitifully
Than Thine, O Christ, on Calvary.

I was making tea in the tent where they,
The wounded, came in their agony;
And the boy turned when his wounds were dressed,
Held up his face like a child at the breast,
Turned and held his tired face up,
For he could not hold the spoon or cup,
And I fed him . . . Mary, Mother of God,
All women tread where thy feet have trod.

And still on the battlefield of pain
Christ is stretched on His Cross again;
And the Son of God in agony hangs,
Womanhood striving to ease His pangs.
For each son of man is a son divine,
Not just to the mother who calls him 'mine',
As he stretches out his stricken hand,
Wounded to death for the Mother Land.

Margaret Sackville

A Memory

There was no sound at all, no crying in the village,
  Nothing you would count as sound, that is, after the
    shells;
Only behind a wall the low sobbing of women,
  The creaking of a door, a lost dog – nothing else.

Silence which might be felt, no pity in the silence,
  Horrible, soft like blood, down all the blood-stained
    ways;
In the middle of the street two corpses lie unburied,
  And a bayoneted woman stares in the market-place.

Humble and ruined folk – for these no pride of
    conquest,
  Their only prayer: 'O! Lord, give us our daily bread!'
Not by the battle fires, the shrapnel are we haunted;
  Who shall deliver us from the memory of these dead?

Poets from overseas

This section represents experiences of the War from a range of overseas poets. They come from Russia, Germany, France and Italy. Translated from their original languages, the works of these writers give a powerful feeling of the universal nature of war — showing that its horrors are the same whatever your nationality.

Marina Tsvetayeva (Russia)

A White Low Sun

A white low sun, low thunderclouds; and back
behind the kitchen-garden's white wall, graves.
On the sand, serried ranks of straw-stuffed forms
as large as men, hang from some cross-beam.

Through the staked fence, moving about, I see
a scattering: of soldiers, trees, and roads;
and an old woman standing by her gate
who chews on a black hunk of bread with salt.

What have these grey huts done to anger you,
my God? and why must so many be killed?
A train passed, wailing, and the soldiers wailed
as its retreating path got trailed with dust.

Better to die, or not to have been born,
than hear that plaining, piteous convict wail
about these beautiful dark eyebrowed women.
It's soldiers who sing these days. O Lord God.

Translated from the Russian by David McDuff and Jon Silkin

George Trakl (Germany)

Grodek

At nightfall the autumn woods cry out
With deadly weapons, and the golden plains
The deep blue lakes, above which more darkly
Rolls the sun; the night embraces
Dying warriors, the wild lament
Of their broken mouths.
But quietly there in the willow dell
Red clouds in which an angry god resides,
The shed blood gathers, lunar coolness.
All the roads lead to blackest carrion.
Under golden twigs of the night and stars
The sister's shade now sways through the silent copse
To greet the ghosts of the heroes, the bleeding heads;
And softly the dark flutes of autumn sound in the reeds.
O prouder grief! You brazen altars,
Today a great pain feeds the hot flame of the spirit,
The grandsons yet unborn.

1914

Translated from the German by Michael Hamburger

August Stramm (Germany)

Battlefield

Yielding clod lulls iron off to sleep
bloods clot the patches where they oozed
rusts crumble
fleshes slime
sucking lusts around decay.
Murder on murder
blinks
in childish eyes.

January 1915

Translated from the German by Michael Hamburger

Charles Vildrac (France)

Relief

In our place
Fresh troops have come
Sent up the line
As bait for death
Met face to face.

We needed all night to make our escape,
All night and its darkness,
Sweating, frozen, to cross
The martyr forest and its swamp
That shrapnel scourged.

All night in which to crouch,
Then to run like the wind,
Each man picking his moment,
Trusting to nerve and instinct
And his star.

But beyond the last entanglement,
Out of it all, on the firm road,
Met together, with no delays,
In the glow of the first pipes lit,

Then, mates, O lucky winners,
Then what stumbling voluble joy!

That was the joy of shipwrecked men
With hands and knees upon the shore,
Who laugh with an agonized happiness
As they recover their treasure again;

All the treasure of the vast world,
And of memory unplumbed,
And of the thirst that can be quenched,
And even of the pain you feel
In the shoulders since all danger passed.

And the future! Ah, the future!
Now it is smiling, in the dawn:
A future of two long weeks ahead,
In a barn at Neuvilly.

Ah, the appletrees in blossom!
I'll put blossoms into my letters.
I'll go and read in the middle of a field.
I'll go and have a wash in the river.

The man who is marching in front of me
Whistles a song that his neighbour sings
A song that is far away from war:
I hum it too, and savour it.
Yet: to think of those killed yesterday!

But the man who has tripped
Between death's legs and then
Recovers himself and breathes again,
Can only laugh or only weep:
He has not the heart to mourn.

Today's first light makes all too drunk
The man who finds himself alive;
He is weak and is amazed
To be dawdling so along the road.

And if he dreams it is of the bliss
Of taking off his boots to sleep
In a barn at Neuvilly.

Translated from the French by Christopher Middleton

Giuseppe Ungaretti (Italy)

Brothers

What regiment d'you belong to
brothers?

Word shaking
in the night

Leaf barely born

In the simmering air
involuntary revolt
of the man present at his
brittleness

Brothers

Mariano, 11 July 1916

Translated from the Italian by Jonathan Griffin

Non-fiction texts

This is a selection of non-fiction texts – speeches, letters, diary entries. At its heart are the personal accounts of soldiers and nurses, describing their lives at the front.

Lloyd George, 'That is what we are fighting . . .'

In the autumn of 1914 there were many speeches, stoking British morale for the war with Germany. Remember that in these early days, most commentators said that it would all be over by Christmas.

David Lloyd George was Chancellor of the Exchequer at the time of his speech. He became Prime Minister in 1916. He recognises that it will be 'a long job . . . a terrible war', but notice how his argument appeals to a sense of fair play and patriotism and progress: 'the making of a new Europe – a new world'.

Treaties have gone. The honour of nations has gone. Liberty has gone. What is left? Germany. Germany is left! '*Deutschland über Alles!*'

That is what we are fighting – that claim to predominance of a material, hard civilization which, if it once rules and sways the world, liberty goes, democracy vanishes. And unless Britain and her sons come to the rescue it will be a dark day for humanity . . .

They think we cannot beat them. It will not be easy. It will be a long job; it will be a terrible war; but in the end we shall march through terror to triumph. We shall need all our qualities – every quality that Britain and its people possess – prudence in counsel, daring in action, tenacity in purpose, courage in defeat, moderation in victory; in all things faith.

It has pleased them to believe and to preach the belief that we are a decadent and degenerate people. They proclaim to the world through their professors that we are a non-heroic nation skulking behind our mahogany counters, whilst we egg on more gallant races to their destruction. This is a description given of us in Germany – 'a timorous, craven nation, trusting to its Fleet'. I think they are beginning to find their mistake out already – and there are half a million young men of Britain who have already registered a vow to their King that they will cross the seas and hurl that insult to British courage against its perpetrators on the battle-fields of France and Germany. We want half a million more; and we shall get them.

I envy you young people your opportunity. They have put up the age limit for the Army, but I am sorry to say I have marched a good many years even beyond that. It is a great opportunity, an opportunity that only comes once in many centuries to the children of men. For most generations sacrifice comes in drab and weariness of spirit. It comes to you today, and it comes today to us all, in the form of the glow and thrill of a great movement for liberty, that impels millions throughout Europe to the same noble end. It is a great war for the emancipation of Europe from the thraldom of a military caste which has thrown its shadows upon two generations of men, and is now plunging the world into a welter of bloodshed and death. Some have already given their own lives; they have given the lives of those who are dear to them. I honour their courage, and may God be their comfort and their strength. But their reward is at hand; those who have fallen have died consecrated deaths. They have taken their part in the making of a new Europe – a new world. I can see signs of its coming in the glare of the battlefield.

The people will gain more by this struggle in all lands than they comprehend at the present moment. It is true they will be free of the greatest menace to their freedom. That is not all. There is something infinitely greater and more enduring which is emerging already out of this great conflict – a new patriotism, richer, nobler, and more exalted than the old. I see amongst all classes, high and low, shedding themselves of selfishness, a new recognition that the honour of the country does not depend merely on the maintenance of its glory in the stricken field, but also in protecting its homes from distress. It is bringing a new outlook for all classes. The great flood of luxury and sloth which had submerged the land is receding, and a new Britain is appearing. We can see for the first time the fundamental things that matter in life, and that have been obscured from our vision by the tropical growth of prosperity.

May I tell you in a simple parable what I think this war is doing for us? I know a valley in North Wales, between the mountains and the sea. It is a beautiful valley, snug, comfortable, sheltered by the mountains from all the bitter blasts. But it is very enervating, and I remember how the boys were in the habit of climbing the hill above the village to have a glimpse of the great mountains in the distance, and to be stimulated and freshened by the breezes which came from the hilltops, and by the great spectacle of their grandeur. We have been living in a sheltered valley for generations. We have been too comfortable and too indulgent – many, perhaps, too selfish – and the stern hand of fate has scourged us to an elevation where we can see the great everlasting things that matter for a nation – the great peaks we had forgotten, of Honour, Duty, Patriotism, and, clad in glittering white, the great pinnacle of Sacrifice pointing like a rugged finger to Heaven. We shall descend into the valleys again; but as long as the men and women of this generation last, they will carry in their hearts the image of those great mountain peaks whose foundations are not shaken, though Europe rock and sway in the convulsions of a great war.

September 1914

'The Amiens Dispatch'

Newspaper stories in the early days of the War were bland, patriotic and based largely on censored press releases. On 29 August 1914, in a special Sunday afternoon edition, **The Times** published a letter which did not share the usual feelings of over-optimism. It said enthusiastic volunteers had now reduced to a trickle, and that British troops were heavily outnumbered by German soldiers. The letter caused outrage. Questions were raised in the Houses of Parliament. Its 'creator' was sacked . . . And new recruits flocked to join up.

THE TRUTH FROM THE BRITISH ARMY
GERMAN 'TIDAL WAVE'
OUR SOLDIERS OVERWHELMED BY NUMBERS

Amiens Aug. 29

This is a pitiful story I have to write. Would to God it did not fall to me to write it, but the time for secrecy is past. Only by realising what has happened can we nerve ourselves for the effort we must make to retrieve it.

What you know in England may be something like the truth. But I write with the Germans advancing incessantly, while all the rest of France believes they are still held near the frontier . . .

The first inkling I had that the Germans had penetrated far into France was this morning. In a village where a banner inscribed with 'Honour to the British Army' (in English) hung across the road, I met a long Royal Engineers column . . . From some of the men I learned that orders had been received for the British base to be shifted with all possible speed. The Staff had left. The artillery had left . . .

'How is it going?' I inquired of a friendly sergeant. He shrugged his shoulders. At dusk the French were falling back. The tidal wave of German troops which has swept over North-Eastern France will spread still further unless a miracle happens. Our small British force could not stand before a volume so powerful, so immense. It has been scattered all over the country, so I learn from officers – staff officers among them – and men met here and there. The Headquarters staff moved hastily a long way back, and it cannot stay long where it is. As the Captain of the Dragoons said, 'They are everywhere' . . .

I hope I have not been guilty of exaggeration in anything I have written here. I have aimed at telling a plain tale of misfortune and defeat. It is a bitter tale to tell of British troops, but they were set an impossible task. Let us not try to hush up the facts. Let us face them and let them strengthen our resolve to see this war through whatever happens . . .

England should realise and should realise at once that she must send reinforcements, and still send them. Is an army of exhaustless valour to be borne down by the sheer weight of numbers, while young Englishmen at home play golf and cricket? We want men, and we want them now.

Eyewitnesses

The following three texts are drawn from the diaries and letters of two British and one German soldier.

Lieutenant E.H.T. Broadwood, 'The shells began bursting like hail . . .'

Our regiment and the Cheshires with a battery of artillery were sent off to the left of our position in front of a village called Elouges. I got the men of my platoon on a hundred yards, and then – the shells began bursting like hail!

We lay in a potato crop like partridges. I think we were all too petrified to move. We lay just below the crest of a ridge waiting to crawl up to see if any German infantry came along. Before any came we had an order to retire, so that just where my platoon was we did not fire at all. This made it almost more trying, not being able to hit back. We lay under that shellfire for three hours, and I think that none of us will ever forget the feeling of thinking that the next moment we might be dead – perhaps blown to atoms. I kept wondering what it was going to feel like to be dead, and all sorts of little things that I had done, and places I had been to years ago and had quite forgotten, kept passing through my mind. I have often heard of this happening to a drowning man but have never experienced it before and don't want to again. I think you get so strung up that your nerves get into an abnormal condition. My brain seemed extraordinarily cool and collected, which I was proud of, but I looked at my hands and saw them moving and twisting in an extraordinary way, as if they didn't belong to me, and when I tried to use my field glasses to spy at the Germans, it was as much as I could do with the greatest effort to get them up to my eyes, and then I could scarcely see. When the order came to retire, our company got it late.

I could not get some of the men along. They were too dead beat, as it was a broiling day and all the time the sun had been beating on us, but I and a last party of five, climbed up a pear tree and over a garden wall and so, creeping along with the bullets now flying all around, we got over another wall and up a path exposed for a short way. We ran along, and I remember – as an instance of the stupid things one does in moments of excitement – my little hairbrush jumped out suddenly from my haversack and I ran back five or six yards to pick it up – and risked a life for a hairbrush! I found, subsequently, two holes in my haversack where a bullet had passed through, just grazing my clothes, and it may have been then that it went through.

**Gefreiter Fritz Heinemann,
'The enemy let loose . . .'**

Mouquet Farm, 26 September 1916
Suddenly, at half past two, the enemy let loose with devastating drumfire on the position lying in front of us. It was clear the English were preparing to attack. Another man and I ran left and right in order to see whether we had any neighbouring troops on our flanks. We found no one. We quickly prepared for the worst. The situation was not very favourable for we only had our rifles – and no machine-guns or hand grenades. Then came the anxious shouts, 'They're coming!' As

far as we could see the Tommies were moving forward at a trot. Our front line must have been completely torn up by the frightful shelling for we had not heard any rifle or machine-gun fire. Facing the oncoming wave, we could not think of getting up to run to the rear. We would have been shot down like rabbits. And staying to defend the place was as good as committing suicide.

The Tommies soon bypassed our position on both flanks and it wasn't long before we received fire from behind, wounding one man. The English were close enough to throw hand grenades now. After several of them exploded nearby we jumped from our holes and headed for the two dugouts. We quickly scrounged some wood and two overcoats, hanging them in the dugout's entrance to help protect against the flying splinters. I peeked out through the overcoats to observe enemy troops carrying machine-guns and ammunition forward. Two Englishmen walked past within a few feet of the dugout's doorway but did not attempt to enter.

Hours slowly passed in absolute uncertainty. Were we to die, or be taken prisoner? Still, all of us held on to the faint hope that we might be rescued if our own infantry counter-attacked. We had no water and the thirst was unbearable.

Suddenly a tremendous crash shook the dugout, knocking us down and extinguishing the few candles that served as light. A large-calibre shell had fallen directly outside the entrance. We were buried alive! My head ached terribly from the shell's concussion. The air was thick with fumes and difficult to breathe. Since we could no longer hope to escape, one man started yelling and pounding to attract attention. Leutnant Liebau stopped him, explaining that the racket would only start the English shooting.

The man who was wounded twice was the only one among us who could speak English well. He had not lost consciousness so we moved him to the dugout's blocked entrance. Then we began banging on the steps, hoping someone would hear the noise and investigate. Suddenly we heard faint English voices. It was difficult at first for him to shout and hear through the earthen barrier, but he made those on the other side understand that we were completely exhausted and could not dig out by ourselves. With that we heard the sound of shovels hacking away at the ground. Thinking of the fresh air outside, I was flushed with new-found strength and tore at the earth with my hands. In the meantime, Leutnant Liebau collected letters and other papers from the men and ripped them into small pieces. At last, a plate-sized hole was punched through the entrance, letting in light and flooding the dugout with air. Soon the hole was enlarged sufficiently for each of us to crawl out, one after the other. Two soldiers wearing khaki stood waiting with their rifles levelled. Several of our men ignored the weapons upon seeing some grass growing from the wall of the trench. They ripped clumps out and immediately stuffed as much as possible into their mouths. Watching this, one of the enemy soldiers removed his water bottle and passed it around. I will never forget this gesture as long as I live.

Second Lieutenant Cyril Drummond,
'A Boxing Day Smoke'

On Boxing Day we walked up to the village of St Yvon where the observation post was. I soon discovered that places where we were usually shot at were quite safe. There were the two sets of front trenches only a few yards apart and yet there were soldiers, both British and German, standing on top of them, digging or repairing the trench in some way, without ever shooting at each other. It was an extraordinary situation.

In the sunken road I met an officer I knew, and we walked along together so that we could look across to the German front line, which was only about seventy yards away. One of the Germans waved to us and said, 'Come over here.' We said, '*You* come over here if you want to talk.' So he climbed out of his trench and came over towards us. We met, and very gravely saluted each other. He was joined by more Germans, and some of the Dublin Fusiliers from our own trenches came out to join us. No German officer came out, it was only the ordinary soldiers. We talked, mainly in French, because my German was not very good and none of the Germans could speak English well. But we managed to get together all right. One of them said, 'We don't want to kill you, and you don't want to kill us, so why shoot?'

They gave me some German tobacco and German cigars – they seemed to have plenty of those, and very good ones too – and they asked whether we had any jam. One of the Dublin Fusiliers got a tin of jam which had been opened, but very little taken out, and he gave it to a German who gave him two cigars for it. I lined them all up and took a photograph.

Kitty Kenyon, 'A Very Heavy Ward'

In makeshift tents and draughty huts, the Roses of No Man's Land, as they were called, fought another war – against disease, infection, slipping morale and death. These were the nurses and doctors of the front line dealing with wounds that were unimaginably horrific. Here, one nurse recalls life on the ward . . .

We had a very heavy ward and one man was very badly wounded. He was a Scots sergeant-major, an elderly man. He'd lost one eye and he was wounded in his arm and leg. The orderly had to lift him up to have his dressing done, and the Sister and the MO did the dressing together with the orderly and myself lending a hand. It was such a difficult dressing to do. The poor man used to scream. He was the only man I ever knew who did. They were most extraordinarily brave, most of them, absolutely marvellous.

I used to hate it if they died when I was on night duty, because then you had to lay them out yourself. But if they died during the day, the orderlies always did that. My first night duty was on this very heavy ward. There was one man, he'd been a fisherman in civil life and he had dreadful wounds, internal wounds, all fastened up with tubes that ran into a bucket underneath his bed. His bed was up against the door of the marquee, because anyone who was likely to die was always put there so that they could be taken out without fuss and depressing the rest of the wounded. I was terrified that he would die when I was on night duty, and the first thing I used to ask the day nurse when I went on was, 'Is the fisherman still alive?' She said he was, but he was very near death. But as soon as I went in and got into

the marquee he called me and said, 'Sister, can you give
me the drink you gave me last night?' I'd given him
some port warmed with a bit of water and sugar and
he wanted it again. I gave him the drink and I sat with
him.

A little while before he died he opened his eyes and
said, 'You've been an angel to me.' It made me feel
absolutely dreadful. I thought, 'Thank goodness he
doesn't know what I've been thinking, just hoping all
the time that he wouldn't die when I was on duty.' But
he died that night. The night superintendent came in.
She was an elderly Scotswoman, and very kind. She said,
'I'll do the laying out and you hold the lantern for me.'
So we put the screens round and started to lay out this
poor man, ready for the orderlies to take him away. Of
course, the rest of the ward was in darkness and the
men were sleeping, and there was only a dim light and
us behind the screens in this shadowy corner with the
poor, dead soldier. Half-way through, as we turned the
body over, Sister looked at me and shook her head. 'We
do have to do some things, don't we!' she said . . .

. . . The other man I remember very distinctly,
because he was my first real patient. We had been told
there was a convoy coming in. I went off for my tea, and
when I came back again the whole tent was full of huge
men in their overcoats. They were all muddy, some with
bandages, and moving about in the dimness. Sister told
me to attend to a man who was sitting on a bed. He was
a huge Scots sergeant with a very mud-stained, blood-
stained tunic. So I made him lie down on the bed and
cut off his uniform. We had these great, huge scissors
and you simply sliced through the clothing with them. I
gave him a blanket bath and made him tidy and

comfortable. You could tell that he was in terrible pain, and he should really have been a stretcher case.

The first few days he just lay quiet, seldom speaking, gritting his teeth when his dressing was done. But it was a very bad dressing and one day he nearly fainted with the pain of it. Sister, as a joke, said to him that she knew perfectly well he was playing up for a drink of brandy. She turned away from the bed when the dressing was finished and said to me, 'Give him some brandy, Nurse, he really needs it.' I brought the brandy, but he was so furious with Sister that he wouldn't touch it. It stood on his locker all day. He'd been a regular soldier in the Black Watch and had deserted before the war. But on the day war broke out, on 4 August, he'd joined up again with another battalion, and so many were joining at the time that they'd never caught up with him. He'd twice been promoted, and twice been reduced to the ranks.

When he was getting better I remember making his bed one day. There had been something in the papers about the Germans killing prisoners, which had shocked me and I was laying off about how terrible I thought it was. He fell absolutely silent, made no answer at all. It was as if a shutter had come down over his face, and I realized in a flash that he must have done the same thing.

He had a beautiful baritone voice and he used to sing Scottish songs, 'Ye Banks and Braes' and 'Loch Lomond' and 'Bonnie Mary of Argyll'. So I asked him if he would sing 'Annie Laurie' which was a favourite of mine. But he just shook his head. Then I asked him a second time, and after he'd refused twice I knew I mustn't ask again – that it was obviously a song that meant something to him. Then one morning we were doing the dressings. A number of bad cases had come in, and there was one in particular which he must have been able to see that I dreaded doing. It was a very difficult, painful dressing on an arm, and I was helping sister and the MO, handing them things, when suddenly, further down the ward, I heard him singing, very softly. He was singing 'Annie Laurie', and I knew he sang it for me because he saw that I was doing something difficult – so he sang the song I'd asked him to sing. And he never sang it again.

'The Boys are Coming Home'

This persuasive text from 1918 asks the people at home to take practical steps for re-integrating the returning soldiers into a society they had been absent from for several years.

THE BOYS ARE COMING HOME

Every day they are returning from the war, these men who have faced death countless times on the land and sea, and in the air, in the defence of their homes and yours – what are you doing to show your gratitude and appreciation? What are you doing to help these men confronted with the difficult problem of regaining their footing in civil life?

Show your appreciation in a practical way.

It is so easy to praise, cheer, wave flags, but the men who have fought for you don't want empty condolences, and to offer them charity is an insult. They want a chance to become useful civilians again – they want to make good in commerce and industry as they made good in the Army and Navy.

The King's Fund for the Disabled

Fiction texts

This section reminds us of the power of imaginative writers to recreate worlds in stories and novels. Modern fiction has frequently returned to the subject of the First World War, as if, decades later, we are still haunted by the horrors and the suffering. Here, three of our finest contemporary writers show the power of fiction to transport the reader into a world we are too young to have known. The effects – you should be warned – can be horrifyingly real.

Susan Hill, *Strange Meeting*

Susan Hill's 1971 novel is a recreation of life in the trenches for two officers – David Barton and John Hilliard. The title is drawn from Wilfred Owen's poem – one of the many background texts which Susan Hill says she 'read until I could read no more', immersing herself in the details of trench life. In this extract from her novel, Barton and Hilliard discuss the emotional effect the War is having upon them, an attempt through discussion to come to terms with the horrors they have seen.

He woke to a sound which he could not at once identify: it was not only the rain which had already churned up the field outside and soaked under the tent flaps, so that their groundsheets were wet and muddied. There was the soft rumble of water on the canvas. But something else, a tearing noise. He realised that the lamp was on very low, and shaded by a valise which had been propped up on the packing case in front of it.

'Barton?'

'Damn. I'm sorry – I hoped I wouldn't wake you up.'

'What's happened?'

'Nothing and I've nearly finished. Go back to sleep.'

Hilliard stretched. His limbs were cramped and he was damp and chilled. There was the close, mouldy smell of wet grass and soil. The tearing noise had stopped. Barton was sitting down, only the top of his head was visible over the upright valise.

'What are you doing?'

For a moment he did not answer. Then he said, 'I suppose I found out that whatever I'd been trying to achieve didn't work and shouldn't work. I mean that *I ought not to have tried at all.'*

He spoke very quietly but there was a note of despair in his voice.

'I couldn't sleep and I knew why. I'll feel better now. Look, I didn't mean to wake you.'

Hilliard was standing. 'It's not particularly comfortable anyway.'

'No.'

'I'm fairly wet. That would have woken me up before long. I don't seem to be able to be wet though I get through most other disturbances. I slept for six hours in a trench at Ancerre, with half a hundredweight of earth and a dead man on top of me.'

Barton did not comment.

'You can get used to almost anything you know.'

'But should you?'

'Well, it helps to be able to sleep. You have to sleep when you can.'

'I don't mean things like that – sleeping, getting used to the food, the rats and fleas and noise. I mean . . . other things.'

'I know.'

'I thought about you just now. I've been sitting here for a long time, thinking about you. You've had more time to get used to things, haven't you?'

'Some things. Yes.'

'And yet when you went back to England you couldn't sleep, you had nightmares, you couldn't even bear the smell of the roses. It all came back then, the men you'd seen die, the noises and the smells. You hadn't forgotten.' He seemed to be asking for some kind of reassurance, that this was truly so, that Hilliard had remembered, and suffered for it.

'You know I hadn't. I told you – I've told you more than anyone.'

'Yes.'

'David, what *have* you been doing tonight?'

He moved across the tent and looked over the valise at the packing case-table. The green-bound copy of Sir Thomas Browne, and the notebook into which Barton had earlier copied the quotations, lay in a pile, torn into small pieces, the leaves ripped from the binding. There were only a few pages still left intact, he had almost finished when Hilliard woke.

'You can't make a pattern out of it, you cannot read a book and get comfort from fine words, and great thoughts, and you shouldn't bloody well *try.*'

'I don't know . . .'

'I do. I've got to face it, it is wicked and pitiless, it is all one Godawful mess, and how can I sit here and let that man, that great man, lull me into a kind of acquiescence? Be romantic about it? Is that right? Is that how he would want to be used?'

'You were reading the Psalms, too.'

'Yes. Or the Psalms or anything. You asked me if it all "helped". Well, if it did it should not have done so.'

Hilliard sat down on the canvas stool beside him. He said, 'Hasn't your father used anaesthetic? And why do we give the men rum issue?'

'For God's sake . . .'

'Isn't it the same?'

'No'

'I wonder.'

'No, John. It's one thing to numb yourself against some kind of pain, to get up courage for an ordeal. This is different, this is a question of basic attitude. I've been trying to set everything apart, make it grandiose, give it a point and a purpose when there are none.'

'Perhaps the men wouldn't agree with you – not all of them. Coulter thinks there's still a reason for it all, for him it is a just war, he'll go on till he drops.'

'I'm not Coulter.'

'You're not being fair to yourself, all the same.'

But it is all right, Hilliard thought, now it is all right again, at least we are talking, he will let me get through to him. He felt enormous relief and a kind of gratitude.

'I told you about what it was like in the summer and when I went home afterwards. I think that was a good thing, for me anyway, because you made me talk and it was what I needed. I couldn't talk to anyone else.'

'No.'

'I haven't forgotten any of what happened in July, I haven't accepted any of it. But I still feel better for having told you.'

Barton smiled and his face lost its withdrawn, formal expression. 'Oh, you should have been a family doctor, you should be a C.O. or a priest! Except that perhaps you would be too conscientious, and I can see through you like a mirror. You are thinking, "What a good thing it would be if only I could get David to spill it all out, how much better he would feel!" Oh, I'm sorry, John, you've been trying very hard with me.'

'Yes.'

'But I have never felt like this in my life before. You must see that. I haven't known myself. I didn't know what to do.'

'I've felt it. I know.'

'Yes. Perhaps we're alike then?'

Hilliard hesitated. 'No,' he said eventually. 'We're not.

And it's a good thing. It's just that we happen to have had the same responses to a situation.'

'It was going up into the o.p. that day. I saw eleven men killed. I suppose that doesn't seem many to you. It was to me, when there wasn't even anything in particular going on, it was a "routine day". Eleven men. There might have been more only that I didn't see them. And there were all those bodies lying out in the shell craters and they'd been there for weeks, months – I don't know. They were all swollen and black and the flies were all over them. And I had to sit there and draw a *map*. I saw . . .' He stopped.

'What? Tell me.'

'No. No, you don't need me to go on.'

'But it would be best if you did.'

'Haven't you had enough of it all yourself?'

'That isn't the point,' Hilliard said gently, and knew then that he had learned all this from David, learned how to listen and to prompt, and why, even learned a tone of voice. Not long ago he would not have been able to do it. He wondered if there was anything that he had not learned from David.

'But the worst of it has been that I haven't known how to face myself. That Private who was snipered – looking at him I could have wept and wept, he seemed to be all the men who had ever been killed, John. I remember everything about him, his face, his hair, his hands, I can remember how pale his eyelashes were and I thought of how alive he'd been, how much there had been going on inside him – blood pumping round, muscles working, brain saying do this, do that, his eyes looking at me. I thought of it all, how he'd been born and had a family, I thought of everything that had gone into making him – and it wasn't that I was afraid and putting myself in his place down there on the ground. I just wanted him alive again, it seemed the only important thing. I just wanted to stay there and look at him, I couldn't take it in, that he'd been so alive, and then he just lay, spouting out blood and that was that, he was dead, nothing. Or something. I don't know. But dead as far as I could see, his flesh was dead, he'd had all that possibility of life and it was gone. Like Harris. A bloody silly accident. If I hadn't been with Grosse I'd have stayed there, I think I would have lain down and never got up again. I wanted to bury myself. Do something. Only – God, I had to make a map, I had a job to do, so I went and did it and I suppose that took my mind off it. By the time I'd been there an hour and by the time I came back into our dugout, I'd begun to accept it all. I was used to it. A man was dead – eleven men were dead. So? It was happening every day, it was no different because I'd been there. It would go on happening and there was not a thing I could do to stop it. In fact, my being here was helping it continue. I felt nothing then, just nothing any longer. I didn't think I could be unfeeling, but I was. Callous. Counting the bodies in No Man's Land and trying to see if they were ours or theirs, guessing how long they'd been dead as a question of academic interest. I had watched stretcher parties scrape and shovel up what was left of half a dozen men, along with what was left of their meal and the side of the trench. I heard a sergeant tell them to go for more help, to get more tools and put down some duckboards, they weren't making a good enough job of it. They did. They simply did it. And ever since I've heard the shells going over, and thought, that's so many dead, so many wounded, one or two dozen, that's next door, that's the right flank trench, where did that one go, and Oh, Pearce is dead then, I'm sorry to hear that, yes, I'll write to his wife, give me his papers, I'll do the form. Last week, the day I went to the village to see the Q.M.S. – that day it hit me, that I'd been feeling nothing, I'd become entirely callous, I was taking it in and not letting myself think or feel anything. I was reading Sir Thomas Browne in order to abstract it. I've never been so ashamed. You said that you can get used to things.

'I knew that. But although you were cool on the surface that is only because you are made like that – it is only the surface. You'd told me all about the summer, and how you felt when you went home, about what struck you most when other people there talked about the war and how it had to go on and I knew you hadn't forgotten, you didn't stop feeling any of it for a moment. But what was happening to me? What has happened to me?'

He had been tearing and tearing at the paper, the pieces were tiny like confetti in a pile before him. Now, he brushed his arm across them so that they scattered, dropping off the packing case and lying, white as flowers, in the mud.

Hilliard said, 'But you haven't forgotten either. You haven't stopped feeling. You have just told me as much.'

'That boy . . .'

'You can't feel every man's death completely and all of the time, David, you simply cannot.'

'Every man's death diminishes me.'

'Yes. So you have just told me the truth, haven't you?'

'Have I?'

'That you are diminished and know as much. And you

are changed. And ashamed. That you feel it. Some people would scarcely have noticed how many men were killed, they've gone past it, it's all become part of the day's work.'

'That was how I felt.'

'No, you didn't, not really. Shock does strange things, you should know that. Some men do not even suffer shock.'

'What kind of men are those?'

'Precisely. But all the same, you know as well as I do that if you are here and doing this job, you have to shove things out of the way all the time. We'd never carry on at all otherwise.'

'Then I wonder if we ought to "carry on at all"?'

'If you truly believe that you can go and say so to Garrett tomorrow, register as a conscientious objector – lay down your arms. I imagine it would be hard – it was hard enough for your brother, and he hadn't gone through the business of joining up and serving. But if that is what you feel, then you must do it.'

Barton looked up. 'It would be funk, wouldn't it? I went through all that before I came out here. It would be funk.'

'You hadn't seen anything then.'

'All the more reason why it would be funk and seen to be so.'

'Are you afraid of what else is to come?'

'I'm afraid of myself. Of what I am becoming, of what it will do to me.'

'Are you afraid of your own dying?'

Barton's face lightened at once. 'Oh, no. I've thought about that too. No. I have never really been afraid of that.'

'It is a brave act of valour to condemn death, but where life is more terrible, it is the truest valour to live.'

Barton smiled. 'I've just torn all that up.'

'But I have just learned it by heart.'

'And is it true?' Hilliard considered. But he found himself thinking instead, whatever was wrong between us is wrong no longer, and will never be so again. He was certain of that.

He said, 'It isn't going to get any better. It is not going to stop being more terrible. None of that nonsense about its all being over and done with by Christmas, about our driving them out like foxes from cover. I scarcely believe that it will ever be over. At any rate there is no point in thinking so.'

'But I asked you if it were true that where life is more terrible it is the truest valour to live.'

'Isn't it something you have to make up your own mind about?'

'Is it true for you, then?'

'Yes,' Hilliard said, 'it's true. I think so. And you?'

'I don't know.'

Barton was looking down at the scattered shreds of paper. 'What a philosophical night!'

'No. We have been talking about what is happening, about yesterday and today and tomorrow.'

'Yes. Do you suppose I ought to gather up the remains of Sir Thomas Browne?'

'He's stuck in the mud.'

'A sort of burial. Fitting.'

'Yes. Though as a matter of fact I'm rather sorry. I wanted to borrow the book and read it for myself.'

Barton stood up and put his arm across Hilliard's shoulders, his face suffused with amusement. 'Don't

worry. I've got another copy at home. I'll get my mother
to send it out to us!'

'Do that.'

A gust of wind blew the tent flap open, blew rain
inside.

'It's going to be bloody wet and bloody cold,' Hilliard
said looking down at his groundsheet. They ought to
finish their sleep, though he had no idea of the time.

Barton let his arm drop, and moved a pace away. He
said, 'I love you, John.'

Hilliard looked at him. 'Yes.' He was amazed at
himself. That it was so easy.

'Yes.'

Pat Barker, *The Ghost Road*

Pat Barker's 1995 novel won the Booker Prize for fiction. It tells the story of Lieutenant Billy Prior who is returning to France after being treated at Craiglockhart War Hospital for 'shell-shock' – the psychological illness suffered by many soldiers as a result of war. Back in France, with his fellow victim, Wilfred Owen, he keeps a diary of the ongoing horrors. Readers are warned that some details in the extract are shocking.

5 October

I think the worst time was after the counter-attack, when we lay in that trench all day surrounded by the dead. I still had Longstaffe by my side, though his expression changed after death. The look of surprise faded. And we listened to the wounded groaning outside. Two stretcher-bearers volunteered to go out and were hit as soon as they stood up. Another tried later. After that I said, No more, everybody keep down. By nightfall most of the groaning had stopped. A few of the more lightly wounded crawled in under cover of darkness and we patched them up as best we could. But one man kept on and on, it didn't sound like a human being, or even like an animal, a sort of guttural gurgling like a blocked drain.

I decided I ought to try myself, and took Lucas with me. Not like going over the top used to be, *climbing* out of the bloody trench. Just a quick slither through the wire, barbs snagging the sleeves, and into the mud. I felt the coldness on my cheek, and the immense space above, that sense you always get when lying on the ground in the open of the earth as a ball turning in

space. There was time to feel this, in spite of the bullets
– which anyway frightened me less than the thought of
having to see what was making that sound.

The gurgling led us to him. He was lying half way
down the side of a flooded crater and the smell of gas
was stronger here, as it always is near water. As we
started down, bullets peppered the surface, *plop, plop,
plop*, an innocent sound like when you skim a flat stone
across a river, and bullets flicked the rim where we'd
been a second before and sent cascades of loose earth
down after us. The gurgling changed as we got closer so
he knew something different was happening. I don't
think he could have known more than that. I got right
up to his feet, and started checking his legs for wounds,
nothing, but then I didn't expect it. That sound only
comes from a head wound. What made it marginally
worse was that the side of the head nearest me was
untouched. His whole frame was shaking, his skin blue
in the starlight as our skins were too, but his was the
deep blue of shock. I said 'Hallet' and for a second the
gurgling stopped. I gestured to Lucas and he helped me
turn him further over on to his back, and we saw the
wound. Brain exposed, a lot of blood, a lot of stuff not
blood down the side of the neck. One eye gone. A hole
– I was going to say *in* his left cheek – where his left
cheek had been. Something was burning, casting an
orange light into the sky which reflected down on us.
The farm that had been one of our reference points.
The underside of the clouds was stained orange by the
flames.

We got a rope underneath him and started hauling
him round the crater, up the other side, towards our
trench and all the time I was thinking, What's the use?

He's going to die anyway. I think I thought about killing him. At one point he screamed and I saw the fillings in his back teeth and his mouth filled with blood.
After that he was quiet, and it was easier but then a flare went up and everything paled in the trembling light. Bastards, bastards, bastards, I thought. I heard a movement and there on the rim of the crater was a white face looking down. Carter, who, I later discovered, had come out entirely on his own initiative. That was just right. More than three and we'd have been getting in each other's way. We managed to drag him back through fire that was, if anything, lighter than before, though not intentionally I think. Too little mercy had been shown by either side that day for gestures of that sort to be possible.

We fell into the trench. Hallet on top of us. I got something damp on my face that wasn't mud, and brushing it away found a gob of Hallet's brain between my fingertips. Because he'd gone quiet on the last stretch I expected to find him unconscious or dead, but he was neither. I gave him a drink of water. I had to press my hand against his face to get it down, because otherwise it slopped out of the hole. And all the time I was doing it I was thinking, Die can't you? For God's sake, man, just *die*. But he didn't.

When at last we were ordered to pull back I remember peering up at the sky and seeing the stars sparse and pale through a gauze of greenish light, and thinking. Thank God it's evening, because shells were still coming over, and some of them were falling directly on the road. At least we'd be marching towards the relative safety of night.

The sun hung on the lip of the horizon, filling the

sky. I don't know whether it was the angle or the drifting
smoke that half obscured it, but it was *enormous*. The
whole scene looked like something that couldn't be
happening on earth, partly the sun, partly the utter
lifelessness of the land around us, pitted, scarred,
pockmarked with stinking craters and scrawls of
barbed-wire. Not even birds, not even carrion feeders.
Even the crows have given up. And I stumbled along at
the head of the company and I waited for the sun to go
down. And the sodding thing didn't. IT ROSE. It wasn't
just me. I looked round at the others and I saw the same
stupefaction on every face. We hadn't slept for four
days. Tiredness like that is another world, just like noise,
the noise of a bombardment, isn't like other noise. You
see people wade through it, lean into it. I honestly think
if the war went on for a hundred years another language
would evolve, one that was capable of describing the
sound of a bombardment or the buzzing of flies on a
hot August day on the Somme. There are no words.
There are no words for what I felt when I saw the setting
sun rise.

6 October

We're far enough back now for officers from different
companies to mess together again. I sit at a rickety little
table censoring letters, for the post has arrived, including one for me from Sarah saying she isn't pregnant. I
don't know what I feel exactly. I ought to be delighted
and of course I am, but that was not the first reaction.
There was a split second of something else, before the
relief set in.

Letters arrive for the dead. I check names against the

list and write *Deceased* in a firm bold hand in the top left-hand corner. Casualties were heavy, not so much in the initial attack as in the counter-attacks.

Gregg died of wounds. I remember him showing me a letter from home that had big 'kisses' in red crayon from his little girl.

Of the people who shared the house in Amiens only a month ago, Potts is wounded, but likely to live. Jones (Owen's servant) wounded, likely to live. Hallet's wounds are so bad I don't think he can possibly survive. I see him sometimes lying in the lily pond in the garden with the golden fish darting all around him, and silver lines of bubbles on his thighs. More like a pattern than a picture, no depth to it, no perspective, but brilliantly clear. And Longstaffe's dead.

The Thane of Fife had a wife: where is she now?

I look across at Owen, who's doing casualty reports with a Woodbine – now blessedly plentiful again – stuck to his bottom lip, and his hair, rather lank at the moment, flopping over his forehead. For days after the battle he went round with his tunic stiff with blood, but then I had blood and brains on me. We must have stunk like the drains in a slaughterhouse, but we've long since stopped smelling each other. He looks like one of the boys you see on street corners in the East End. Open to offers. I must say I wouldn't mind. He looks up, feeling himself the subject of scrutiny, smiles and pushes the fags across. I saw him in the attack, caped and masked in blood, seize a machine-gun and turn it on its previous owners at point-blank range. Like killing fish in a bucket. And I wonder if he sees those faces, grey, open-mouthed faces, life draining out of them before the bullets hit, as I see the faces of the men I killed in the counter-attack. I won't ask. He wouldn't answer if I did. I wouldn't *dare* ask . . .

We don't even mention our own dead. The days pass crowded with meaningless incident, and it's easier to forget. I run the ball of my thumb against the two first fingers of my right hand where a gob of Hallet's brain was, and I don't feel anything very much.

We are Craiglockhart's success stories. *Look at us.* We don't remember, we don't feel, we don't think – at least not beyond the confines of what's needed to do the job. By any proper civilized standard (but what does *that* mean *now?*) we are objects of horror. But our nerves are completely steady. And we are still alive.

Sebastian Faulks, *Birdsong*

Sebastian Faulks' novel, published in 1993, traces the history of Stephen Wraysford as he drifts from domestic life in France to the agonising realities of life as a lieutenant in the First World War, and the horrors of the Somme. The book has been highly praised for the way it evokes the details of the War. In this extract, Captain Michael Weir, Stephen's friend, is on leave, and returns unannounced to his family in the Midlands. Their reactions clearly show that they have no interest in hearing the realities of life at the front.

Weir had been on leave to England. He arrived at dusk at his parents' Victorian villa in Leamington Spa and rang the front door bell. The maid opened it and asked him who he was. His telegram had gone astray; they were not expecting him. His mother was out, but the maid told him she thought his father would be in the garden. It was an October evening, three months after they had attacked on the Ancre.

Weir took off his greatcoat and left it on a chair in the hall. He dropped his kitbag on the floor and made his way through to the back of the house. There was a large flat lawn with laurel bushes and a giant cedar in one corner. He saw the gnats in the damp air ahead of him and felt his boots sink into the short-cropped lawn. The packed grass gave luxurious support to his steps. The air was thick with garden scents at evening. The denseness of the silence pressed his ears. Then he heard a door bang in the house, he heard a thrush; then a motor lorry backfiring in the quiet suburban street.

On the left of the lawn was a large greenhouse. Weir could make out a trickle of smoke coming from the door. As he approached it he caught the familiar smell of his father's pipe tobacco. He stood in the doorway and looked inside. His father was kneeling beneath a shelf on which small boxes of seeds were neatly laid out. He appeared to be talking to someone.

'What are you doing?' said Weir.

'Feeding the toad,' said his father, without looking up. 'Quiet now.'

From an old tobacco tin on the ground beside him, he took a small dead insect, pinched it between finger and thumb and pushed his hand slowly forwards under the shelf. Weir could see the polished seat of his trousers and the back of his bald head, but little else.

'That's it, that's my beauty. He's a champion, this one. You should see the size of him. We've not had an insect in here for weeks. Come and have a look at him.'

Weir went over the uncemented paving that his father had laid down the middle of the greenhouse and knelt on the gravel next to him.

'You see there? In the corner?'

Weir heard a fat croak from the direction his father indicated. 'Yes,' he said. 'A fine specimen.'

His father backed out from under the seed boxes and stood up. 'You'd better come on in then. Your mother's at choir practice. Why didn't you let us know you were coming?'

'I sent a telegram. It must have got lost. I didn't know until the day itself.'

'Well, never mind. We've had your letters. Maybe you'll want a wash after your journey.'

Weir looked across at his father's portly figure as they walked over the lawn. He wore a cardigan over his shirt, still with its stiff collar from the day at the office, and a dark, striped tie. Weir wondered if he was going to say any word of greeting. By the time they reached the french windows to the sitting room it was clear that the moment had passed.

His father said, 'I'll get the maid to make up a bed if you're stopping.'

'If that's all right,' said Weir. 'Just for a night or two.'

'Of course it's all right.'

Weir took his kitbag upstairs and went to the bathroom. The water roared in the pipes, stalled, gurgled with an airlock that shook the room, then thundered from the wide mouth of the tap. He dropped his clothes on the floor and sank into the bath. He expected that he would soon feel at home. He went to his old room and dressed carefully in flannel trousers and checked shirt: he was waiting for the moment when the familiar wash of normality would come over him and he would be restored to his old self; when the experiences of the last two years would recede into some clear perspective. He noticed that the clothes were too big on him. The trousers rested on his hip bones. He found some braces in a drawer and hitched them up. Nothing happened. The polished mahogany of the chest looked alien; it was hard to imagine that he had seen it before. He went to the window and looked down on the familiar view, where the garden ended by the cedar tree and the corner of the next-door house with its rear terrace and long drainpipe blocked the skyline. He remembered afternoons of childhood boredom when he had looked out at this view, but the familiar recollection did not bring back any sense of belonging.

When he went downstairs he found his mother had returned.

She kissed him on the cheek. 'You look a bit thin,

Michael,' she said. 'What have they been feeding you on over in France?'

'Garlic,' he said.

'Well no wonder!' She laughed. 'We got your letters. Very nice they were, too. Very reassuring. When was the last one we had?'

'About a fortnight ago. You'd moved, you said.' Weir's father was standing by the fireplace, loading another pipe.

'That's right,' said Weir. 'We moved up from Beaucourt. We're moving again soon, up towards Ypres. Near somewhere called Messines, where we were at the start. I'm not really supposed to tell you too much.'

'I wish we'd known you were coming,' said his mother. 'We had our tea early so I could go to choir practice. There's a bit of cold ham and tongue if you're hungry.'

'That would be nice.'

'All right. I'll get the maid to set it out in the dining room.'

'You're too late for my tomatoes, I'm afraid,' said his father. 'We had a champion crop this year.'

'I'll ask the girl if she can find a bit of lettuce.'

Weir ate the meal alone in the dining room. The maid set a place with a glass of water and a clean napkin. There was a slice of bread and butter on the side-plate. He swallowed quietly, the sound of his own chewing magnified by the lack of conversation.

Afterwards he played cards with his parents in the sitting room until ten o'clock when his mother said it was time for her to go to bed.

'It's nice to see you all in one piece, Michael,' she said, as she gathered her cardigan around her and went to the door. 'Don't you two sit up talking all night.'

Weir sat facing his father across the fireplace.

'How's the office?'

'It's all right. The business doesn't vary as much as you'd think.'

There was a silence. Weir could think of nothing to say.

'We'll ask some people over if you like,' said his father. 'If you're stopping till the weekend.'

'All right. Yes.'

'I expect you'd like a bit of company after all . . . after, you know.'

'France?'

'Exactly. Make a change.'

'It's been terrible,' said Weir. 'I've got to tell you, it's been – '

'We've read about it in the paper. We all wish it would hurry up and finish.'

'No, it's been worse. I mean, you can't imagine.'

'Worse than what? Worse than it says? More casualties, are there?'

'No, it's not that. It's . . . I don't know.'

'You want to take it easy. Don't get yourself upset. Everyone's doing their bit, you know. We all want it to end, but we just have to get on with things in the meantime.'

'It isn't that,' said Weir. 'It's . . . I wonder if I could have a drink?'

'A drink? What of?'

'A . . . glass of beer, perhaps.'

'We haven't any in. There might be some sherry in the cupboard, but you wouldn't want that, would you? Not at this time of night.'

'No. I suppose not.'

Weir's father stood up. 'You get yourself a good
night's sleep. That's the best thing. I'll ask the maid to
get some beer tomorrow. We've got to build you up
after all.'

He put out his hand and patted his son on the back
of the left bicep.

'Good night, then,' he said. 'I'll lock up.'

'Good night,' said Weir.

When he could no longer hear his father's footsteps
upstairs, he went to the corner cupboard and took out
the two-thirds-full bottle of sherry. He went out into the
garden and sat on a bench where he lit a cigarette and
raised the bottle in his trembling hand.

Visions of the Great War

Empty lines: Abandoned British trenches zigzagging across Tiescault, France, December 1917

Trench congestion: Australian soldiers relax 15 feet below ground, Ypres 1917

Opposite   The front-line: A soldier keeps watch while his mates rest, Battle of the
Somme 1916

Icy look-out: A sentry of the 12th East Yorkshires keeps watch from the firestep near Roclincourt, January 1918

Opposite Over the top: Soldiers clamber into No Man's Land, Battle of the Somme, 1916

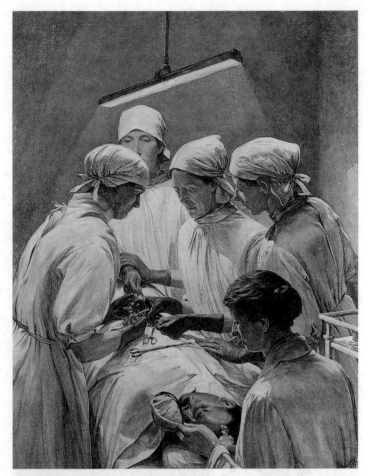

The fight for life: War-artist Francis Dodd's impression of an operation at a military hospital

Opposite Across the wire: The first day of the Battle of the Somme, 1 July 1916

Aftermath: German trenches destroyed in the Battle of the Somme, Ovillers, July 1916

Waterlogged: The shattered landscape of Passchendaele after battle, 1917

☐ Afterwords

Laurence Binyon's 'For the Fallen' and Philip Larkin's 'MCMXIV' are two poems that sum up many of the feelings people have today about the events of the Great War. Laurence Binyon's poem is probably the most frequently quoted of all First World War texts, used on state occasions as a tribute to the people who died in the War. Its language echoes the archaic phrasing associated with other early voices of the War.

Larkin's poem is the most recent in this collection. Written in 1960, it attempts to come to terms with the way people signed up so cheerfully and so unquestioningly to fight for their country. Where Binyon's poem expresses certainty, pride and powerful rhetoric, Larkin's is questioning, part fascinated and part astonished at the apparent innocence of a world now lost.

Together the poems capture the range of feelings most of us have as we respond to the various voices of the Great War.

Laurence Binyon

For the Fallen

With proud thanksgiving, a mother for her children,
England mourns for her dead across the sea.
Flesh of her flesh they were, spirit of her spirit,
Fallen in the cause of the free.

Solemn the drums thrill: Death august and royal
Sings sorrow up into immortal spheres.
There is music in the midst of desolation
And a glory that shines upon our tears.

They went with songs to battle, they were young,
Straight of limb, true of eye, steady and aglow,
They were staunch to the end against odds uncounted,
They fell with their faces to the foe.

They shall grow not old, as we that are left grow old:
Age shall not weary them, nor the years condemn.
At the going down of the sun and in the morning
We will remember them.

They mingle not with their laughing comrades again;
They sit no more at familiar tables at home;
They have no lot in our labour of the day-time;
They sleep beyond England's foam.

But where our desires are and our hopes profound,
Felt as a well-spring that is hidden from sight,
To the innermost heart of their own land they are
    known
As the stars are known to the Night.

As the stars that shall be bright when we are dust,
Moving in marches upon the heavenly plain,
As the stars that are starry in the time of our darkness,
To the end, to the end, they remain.

1914

Philip Larkin

MCMXIV

Those long uneven lines
Standing as patiently
As if they were stretched outside
The Oval or Villa Park,
The crowns of hats, the sun
On moustached archaic faces
Grinning as if it were all
An August Bank Holiday lark;

And the shut shops, the bleached
Established names on the sunblinds,
The farthings and sovereigns,
And dark-clothed children at play
Called after kings and queens,
The tin advertisements
For cocoa and twist, and the pubs
Wide open all day;

And the countryside not caring:
The place-names all hazed over
With flowering grasses, and fields
Shadowing Domesday lines
Under wheat's restless silence;
The differently-dressed servants
With tiny rooms in huge houses,
The dust behind limousines;

Never such innocence,
Never before or since,
As changed itself to past
Without a word – the men
Leaving the gardens tidy,
The thousands of marriages
Lasting a little while longer:
Never such innocence again.

1960

Glossary

This section includes questions on individual poems and starting-points for comparing texts.

Thomas Hardy

Channel Firing

This poem is typical of Hardy's style: note that it is being spoken by the awakened dead of a graveyard!

2 *chancel*   the eastern end of a church containing the altar.

drearisome   mournful, sad.

glebe   land belonging to the church.

blow the trumpet   i.e. to signal the end of the world.

3 *indifferent*   unfeeling.

Men Who March Away

4 *purblind*   foolish.

dolorous   sad.

hoodwink   trick.

Dalliers   time-wasters.

rueing   regretting.

5 *braggarts*   boasters.

The Dead and the Living One

6 *concave*   inward curve.

   countenance   face.

   plaintive   sorrowful.

   blandishment   flattery.

7 *repose*   rest.

   Adieu   (French) goodbye.

   lament   mourn.

A New Year's Eve in War Time

8 *Phantasmal*   ghostly.

   gable-cock   weathercock showing the direction of the wind.

9 *Severance*   separation.

   intone   wail.

Rudyard Kipling

Gethsemene

11 *The Garden called Gethsemene*   the place where Christ was betrayed by Judas on the night before his crucifixion.

   Picardy   a flat area of northern France, scene of heavy fighting.

A Song in Storm

12 *jeopardy*   danger.

   combers   long rolling waves.

   leagued   joined together.

   whelm   cover up.

13 **rebuke**   reject.

billow   gust of wind.

baulked   halted.

Mesopotomia

14 **Mesopotomia**   scene of a lengthy campaign (November 1914–October 1918) by British and Indian soldiers to protect the oil supplies of Iraq.

resolute   determined.

overlings   those responsible for the running of the War.

quibbled   argued over trivial matters.

contrivance   scheming.

The Verdicts

16 **Jutland**   a major naval battle between Britain and Germany, off the coast of Denmark, 31 May–1 June 1916. Although the battle proved indecisive, it is usually seen as a British victory because the German fleet never again ventured out of port except on minor sorties. Kipling's poem celebrates the heroism of the British fighters.

demi-gods   half human beings, half gods.

appraise   calculate.

A Death-bed

17 **'Regis suprema voluntas Lex'**   (Latin) 'The Law is the supreme will of the King'.

Rupert Brooke

I Peace

20 *Naught* nothing.

III The Dead

22 *serene* tranquillity; peace.

immortality everlasting fame.

dearth (in this context) lack of these qualities.

Comparisons

1 What similarities and differences do you notice between Hardy, Kipling and Brooke:
   - in their attitudes to the War, for example, who seems the most critical?
   - in their written styles, who seems most poetic?

2 Which poem:
   - contains most emotion?
   - contains most factual information about the War?
   - seems most traditional in the way it is written?
   - contains vocabulary which feels most distant from our own times?

3 Which poem do you like most? Say why.

Siegfried Sassoon

A Night Attack

25 rank rotten.

Bosche (French slang) abusive term, used during the War by British soldiers when referring to Germans; also spelt 'Boche'.

26 Prussian German. Until the German Republic was established in 1871, Prussia was the mightiest military power in Europe. It then became a state within the German Empire.

'hows' short for howitzers – cannons.

Twelve Months After

27 impassive not revealing any emotions.

D.C.M the Distinguished Conduct Medal: a military honour for bravery.

fide Sassoon represents the accents of the soldiers, writing 'fide' for 'fade'; similarly, 'a-why' means 'away'.

The General

28 Arras scene of a battle in April 1917.

The Dug-Out

29 ungainly awkwardly.

sullen sulky.

Aftermath

30 Mametz scene of fierce fighting during the Battle of the Somme (1916).

parapets the top edge of trenches.

Comparisons

1 What are your immediate impressions of Siegfried Sassoon's poetry and the way it differs from the 'Early voices'? You might consider:
   - the subject matter of the poems
   - the attitude to war and its leaders
   - the writer's style.

2 Which poem seems:
   - most emotional
   - most factual
   - most personal
   - most complex
   - most straightforward?

3 Which do you like or admire most? Say why.

Isaac Rosenberg

Break of Day in the Trenches

32 **druid**   priest from pre-Christian times. Rosenberg uses the image to suggest that time has always been like this – perhaps one of the few reassuringly stable elements in his life.

sardonic   mockingly funny.

cosmopolitan   free from national prejudices – the joke is that the rat happily moves between the trenches of the different nationalities.

haughty   proud.

whims   casual decisions.

aghast   horrified.

GLOSSARY

Louse Hunting

33 *lurid*   unnaturally vivid.

lice   bloodsucking insects – one of the many discomforts soldiers had to endure.

gargantuan   huge.

smutch   smudge, though perhaps here to squeeze.

Highland fling   a fast-paced dance from Scotland.

revel   dance.

Returning, We Hear the Larks

34 *anguished*   suffering.

The Dying Soldier

35 *swooned*   collapsed.

Dead Man's Dump

36 *limbers*   part of a gun, consisting of an axle, pole and two wheels, which is attached to transport it.

sceptres   ornate staffs held by kings and queens as a symbol of their power and majesty.

stay   used here as a verb: to hold back.

Fretting   worrying, anxious.

God-ancestralled essences   Rosenberg's grim fantasy asks whether the souls of the men are totally cut off from the influence of God.

37 *pyre*   funeral fire for the cremation of a corpse.

ichor   in Greek mythology this is the fluid said to run through the veins of the gods. In medicine, it is the foul-smelling discharge from a wound.

pangs   sudden sharp feelings.

impetuous   acting suddenly without thinking ahead.

Comparisons

1   What are your impressions of Rosenberg's poetry after reading the earlier sections of this collection? Does he feel more graphic, more angry, more emotional, more descriptive, more poetic?

2   How does Rosenberg use imagery to make his subject powerfully memorable? Find some examples of images which you think create a particularly strong effect.

3   Which poem in this section is:
   • most memorable
   • most depressing
   • most complex
   • most emotional?

Wilfred Owen

Anthem for Doomed Youth

40   *orisons*   prayers.

shires   counties of Britain (e.g. Shropshire, Herefordshire, Kent).

demented   mad.

pallor   paleness.

Strange Meeting

41   *titanic*   huge.

groined   an architectural term describing the meeting of two vaults, as in the ceilings of large churches, but here seeming closer to the origin of the word: ground or grind.

encumbered   hindered.

42 cess   sewage.

parried   from the sport of fencing, meaning to ward off an attack, fight back.

Dulce et Decorum Est

43 Five-Nines   explosive shells.

ardent   eager.

Dulce et decorum . . . mori   (Latin) a quotation from the Roman poet, Horace, meaning 'sweet and honourable it is to die for your country'.

Futility

44 Futility   lack of purpose or meaning.

fatuous   pointless.

Disabled

46 jewelled hilts   decorated handles of daggers. In other words, the boy thinks of the glorious trappings of war.

plaid   tartan patterned.

Esprit de corps   team spirit.

Exposure

47 salient   the point where the forward line projects out towards enemy territory.

melancholy   gloomy.

nonchalance   uncaring attitude.

48 glozed   glossy or glazed.

invincible   unconquerable.

The Sentry

49 ***Boche***   see note to page 25.

deluging   overflowing.

Comparisons

1   What range do you notice in Owen's poetry? Does it vary in its emotional content, in its attitude to war, in its written style?

2   Which poem seems:
- most angry
- most factual
- most complex
- most straightforward
- most personal
- most emotional?

3   Which do you particularly like or admire? Why?

Edmund Blunden

The Zonnebeke Road

52 ***Zonnebeke***   a village between two of the great First World War battlefields, Ypres and Passchendaele.

kindred   connection, relationship.

seeming-saturnine   appearing gloomy.

Haymarket   the nickname British soldiers gave to a trench near the Zonnebeke Road. It comes from the name of the famous street in London's West End.

minenwerfers   small missiles which would hang in the air before dropping.

gargoyle   ugly sculpted face on the side of a church or tower.

bine   stem of a climbing plant (a reminder of Blunden's closeness to nature and its precise terms).

53 *Ypres*   scene of three major battles in 1914, 1915 and 1917.

disdain   contempt; strong dislike.

Third Ypres

54 *Third Ypres*   the Third Battle of Ypres, July 1917, also known as Passchendaele. A heavy bombardment of German bases was mounted, using four million shells. The bombardment churned up the ground. Heavy rain fell. Dirt turned to mud. Soldiers were expected to advance and fight in impossible conditions. The result: 370,000 British dead and wounded.

fascined   a fascine is a long bundle of sticks used for lining ditches and trenches.

parley   discussion between enemies. Here it is the guns of the opposing sides which hold the conversation.

55 *unplashed hedge*   a hedge that has been allowed to grow wild.

56 *pollard*   a tree on which the branches have been heavily trimmed.

57 *lyddite*   explosive used in shells.

amuck   frenzied; alive with.

The Ancre at Hamel: Afterwards

59 *Hamel*   village of Beaumont Hamel on the River Ancre, scene of fierce fighting during the Battle of the Somme, 1916.

1916 Seen from 1921

60 *seared*   scorched.

Comparisons

1 More than any other poet in this collection, Blunden is a nature poet. What do you notice in his various poems about his attitude to nature?

2 How does the tone of Blunden's poetry seem different from any of the other poets you have read?

3 Which poem in this section did you:
   - most enjoy
   - find most emotional
   - find most straightforward
   - find most complex
   - find most factual?

Poems by women

63 Conscientious Objector

Conscientious Objector   someone for whom war is so strongly against their principles that they refuse to serve in the armed forces. They were often sent to the front line in other roles instead – such as medical support.

Cuba   island in the West Indies, at the entrance to the Gulf of Mexico.

Balkans   the countries of the former Yugoslavia, Rumania, Bulgaria, Albania, Greece and part of Turkey, where technically the First World War began.

bridle   headgear for a horse.

cinches the girth   fasten the saddle to a horse by tying a strap around its stomach. All the horse imagery here implies power and domination: the writer's point is that she is not prepared to help the rider to achieve it.

Perhaps —

64 *bereft*   deprived, usually by the death of someone.

Lamplight

65 *laborious*   tedious.

The Falling Leaves

67 *gallant multitude*   courageous group.
   Flemish   Belgian.

An Incident

69 *Calvary*   the place outside Jerusalem where Christ was crucified.
   pangs   sudden bursts of pain.
   divine   holy.
   stricken   weakened.

Comparisons

1   What aspects of the experience of war do the women writers illuminate which are not present in the other sections?

2   Which of the poems in this section do you most like or admire? Why?

3   Which poem is:
   • most factual
   • most emotional
   • most interesting
   • most poetic
   • most complex
   • most straightforward?

Poets from overseas

A White Low Sun

72 *serried*   tightly organised.

Grodek

73 *lament*   song of mourning.
   carrion   dead flesh.
   brazen   shameless.

Battlefield

74 *clod*   lumps of earth.

Relief

75 *martyr forest*   i.e. an innocent victim of the war.
   voluble   babbling – the relief of speech after hours of silence.

Brothers

78 *involuntary*   uncontrollable.

Comparisons

1   Which of the poems do you find particularly memorable or
    interesting? Why?
2   Are there any clues in the poems that they were written
    by poets from overseas – in their content or style?

Non-fiction texts

Lloyd George, 'That is what we are fighting . . .'

80 ***Deutschland über Alles*** 'Germany over everyone' – the refrain
of the German national anthem.

decadent and degenerate idle and wasteful.

skulking hiding away.

81 ***timorous*** timid, nervous.

craven cowardly.

emancipation liberation, freedom.

consecrated sacred, because they were fighting for a just cause.

82 ***scourged*** whipped.

pinnacle peak.

83 ***convulsions*** violent upheavals.

'The Amiens Dispatch'

84 ***incessantly*** without stopping.

valour bravery.

borne down defeated.

Gefreiter Fritz Heinemann, 'The enemy let loose . . .'

87 ***Tommies*** (slang) British soldiers.

concussion temporary unconsciousness.

Kitty Kenyon, 'A Very Heavy Ward'

90 ***marquee*** makeshift tent, erected for use as a hospital.

'The Boys are Coming Home'

93 condolences expressions of sympathy.

Comparisons

1 These non-fiction texts all show different perspectives on the War. What new factual information have you learnt from reading them?

2 What picture do you gain of the different writers of the extracts? Compare two or three of the narrators.

3 Which text do you find:
   - most informative
   - most interesting
   - most emotional
   - most descriptive
   - most disturbing?

   Explain each of your choices.

Fiction texts

Strange Meeting

95 valise small travelling bag.

97 Sir Thomas Browne (1605–82) philosopher and writer, famous for his witty style.

acquiescence acceptance.

Psalms sacred songs, contained in the Book of Psalms in the Old Testament of the Bible.

98 grandiose (in this context) significant.

C.O. commanding officer.

99 o.p. observation post, used to keep watch over the battlefields.

100 *Callous* cruel.

    No Man's Land the disputed territory between trenches, which both sides hoped to gain.

101 *Q.M.S.* quartermaster sergeant, whose job was to supervise supplies and equipment.

    Every man's death diminishes me from *Devotions* by John Donne (1572–1631), English poet and preacher: 'Any man's death diminishes me, because I am involved in Mankind; And therefore never send to know for whom the bell tolls; it tolls for thee'.

102 *funk* (slang) cowardice.

The Ghost Road

105 *guttural* in the back of the throat.

108 *carrion feeders* birds that live off dead flesh.

    stupefaction blank astonishment.

109 *The Thane of Fife had a wife: where is she now?* from Shakespeare's *Macbeth*; the words of Lady Macbeth who, turned mad by guilt at the murders she has been involved in, walks and talks in her sleep, trying to wash imaginary spots of blood from her hands: 'The Thane of Fife had a wife: where is she now? – What will these hands ne'er be clean?' (Act 5, scene 1, lines 40–1).

    Woodbine brand of cigarette.

Birdsong

111 *Leamington Spa* town in central Warwickshire, England.

    the Ancre river which flows from the Somme; scene of fierce fighting in 1916.

Comparisons

1   What first impressions do you gain of the main characters in each text – Barton and Hilliard; Billy Prior; Michael Weir?

2   How do the three texts use precise details of people and places to bring to life what's happening at the front, and at home in England?

3   Which text do you find:
- most powerful
- most distressing
- most descriptive
- most factual
- most complex
- most straightforward?

Afterwords

For the Fallen

127   *august*   dignified; proud.

desolation   emptiness caused by destruction.

staunch   strong.

MCMXIV

129   *The Oval*   London cricket ground.

Villa Park   football ground belonging to Aston Villa, in Birmingham.

twist   pipe tobacco shaped like a thick lace.

Domesday lines   traces of the traditional English pastures dating back to the land survey (Domesday Book) of 1086.

Comparisons

1 What picture do the two poems give of England and Englishness?

2 What impression do they both give of the men who fought the War?

3 Philip Larkin's poem was written more than forty years after Laurence Binyon's. Are there any clues in the language, or the attitude of the writer, which indicate its later date?

▢ Study programme

Language study

▢ Critic Paul Fussell has said that the English language changed
during the First World War, and that words associated with
the Victorian past – such as *fallen, strife, deeds* – were abandoned by the new generation of War poets. Look back at the
'Early voices' section (page 1) and pay particular attention to
the vocabulary. Look, for example, at the sonnets of Rupert
Brooke and make a list of words which you think feel archaic
or old fashioned. It might be that you notice words used
in deliberately poetic ways – time described as if it were a
person, or nature described for emotional effect.

Then look at one of the other poets of the War – say,
Wilfred Owen or Siegfried Sassoon – and make a list of some
of their vocabulary which feels more contemporary and
direct. Use a table like the one below to log your results and
try to comment as precisely as you can on the reasons for
your choices. Some examples are done for you.

ARCHAIC LANGUAGE		
Poet	Example	Comment
Rupert Brooke	'tears of men and mirth'	repetition of 'm' sounds makes it feel poetic
	'Time's throwing'	time personified – feels like poetry of an older period
	'if these poor limbs die'	'limbs' here seems a slightly vague word – rather than arms or legs

CONTEMPORARY LANGUAGE		
Poet	**Example**	**Comment**
Siegfried Sassoon	'O Jesus, make it stop'	blashphemy gives real feeling of emotion

2. Some poets use the rhythms and rhymes of songs in their work. Look, for example, at Thomas Hardy and Rudyard Kipling. Discuss what effect this has.

3. The following poems all refer to specific battles of the War:

   - Sassoon's 'A Night Attack'
   - Rosenberg's 'Dead Man's Dump'
   - Owen's 'Exposure'
   - Blunden's 'Third Ypres'.

   Look closely at each poem and write about what you learn of the battles they describe. How does each writer use language to create his effects? How do these poems differ from straight factual accounts? Which do you find most powerful?

4. Look at the portrayal of nature in three poems. What images of nature do the different writers use? How is nature presented? Do the writers show nature as glorious, unchanging, idyllic? Or ruined, another victim of human behaviour?

   Compare some early and later writers, and then share your findings with the rest of the group.

5. Choose a poem which has particularly affected you and write about it, describing what you notice about:

   - its vocabulary
   - its structure
   - the way its ideas develop

- whether it uses rhythm and rhyme
- the picture it creates of the War.

Then write about what you particularly admire in the poem.

6. Choose a piece of prose – either fiction or non-fiction – that you have particularly admired. Write a commentary on it, saying what you notice about:

- its characters (if appropriate)
- the world it creates
- its vocabulary
- its mood
- the way it develops
- any special effects – tension, surprises, unexpected phrasing
- the way it involves the reader.

Then write about what you particularly like or admire about the text.

7. Imagery is one technique writers use to bring their subject to life. There are three common forms of imagery:

- **simile** – a direct comparison of one thing with another; for example: 'Bent double, like old beggars under sacks'
- **metaphor** – a comparison which does not rely on 'like' or 'as'; for example: 'From gloom's last dregs . . .' which compares the darkness to the last few particles in a cup or glass to show that the night has almost ended
- **personification** – taking an abstract concept, such as death, fear or hope, and writing as if it were a person; for example: 'And Chance's strange arithmetic/Comes simpler than the reckoning of their shilling', as if the arithmetic belongs to Chance.

Choose one poem and look for ways in which the writer has used imagery to present ideas and pictures in a memorable way. Working in small groups, you could each focus on a different poet's work and compare the extent to which they each use the different forms of imagery.

8 Look at the following first two drafts of Wilfred Owen's 'Anthem for Doomed Youth' and compare them with the finished version on page 40. What changes do you notice in:

- the vocabulary
- the tone of the poem
- its overall meaning?

Discuss why you think Owen made some of the changes, and how he has improved the poem. Are there any changes which you think make it less effective overall?

Anthem for Doomed Youth
First draft

       passing
What ~~minute~~ bells for these who die so fast?
         ~~solemn~~
— Only the monstrous anger of our guns.
Let the majestic insults of their iron mouths
            requiem
    Be as the ~~priest words~~ of their burials.
Of choristers and holy music, none;
      Nor any voice of mourning, save the wail
The long-drawn wail of high far-sailing shells.
              to light
What candles may we hold ~~for~~ these lost? ~~souls?~~
— Not in the hands of boys, but in their eyes
  shine the ~~tapers~~   the holy ~~tapers~~ candles.
Shall/many ~~candles; shine; and I will light them.~~
         ~~holy~~ flames: to
Women's wide-spreaded arms shall be their wreaths,
And pallor of girls' cheeks shall be their palls.
             ~~mortal~~
Their flowers, the tenderness of ~~all men's~~ minds,
              ~~comrades'~~
             rough men's
    each slow
And ~~every~~ Dusk, a drawing-down of blinds.

Second draft

for
Anthem ~~to~~ Dead Youth

What passing-bells for you who die in herds?
                       the
  — Only the monstrous anger of ~~more~~ guns!
  — Only the stuttering rifles' rattled words
Can patter out your hasty orisons.

                                       choirs
No chants for you, nor blame, nor wreaths, nor bells
                                     shells
    Nor any voice of mourning, save the choirs,
And long-drawn sighs
~~The shrill demented choirs of~~ wailing shells;
    And bugles calling for you from sad shires.

What candles may we hold to speed you all?
    Not in the hands of boys, but in their eyes
Shall S   ~~and gleams~~ our
~~Shall~~ shine ~~the~~ holy lights/of ~~long~~ goodbyes.
                  must
The pallor of girls' brows ~~shall~~ be your pall;
                       ~~broken simple frail~~
Your flowers, the tenderness of ~~mortal~~ minds,
                   ~~pain white~~
                   ~~grief wh innocent~~
                   comrades'
And each slow dusk, a drawing-down of blinds.

Comparisons

☐ Look at the suggested text groupings below, and use them to explore further the writers' different portrayals of the War. Compare:

- their attitudes to the War
- the language and style they use
- the amount of detail they give.

Early and Later voices

- Thomas Hardy, 'Men Who March Away'
- Rudyard Kipling, 'The Verdicts'
- Rupert Brooke, 'The Soldier'
- Wilfred Owen, 'Dulce et Decorum Est'
- 'The Boys are Coming Home'

In battle

- Isaac Rosenberg, 'Dead Man's Dump'
- Edmund Blunden, 'Third Ypres'
- Lieutenant E.H.T. Broadwood, 'The shells began bursting like hail . . .'
- Wilfred Owen, 'Dulce et Decorum Est'
- 'The Boys are Coming Home'

Trench life

- Siegfried Sassoon, 'The Dug-Out'
- Isaac Rosenberg, 'Break of Day in the Trenches'
- Gefreiter Fritz Heinemann, 'The enemy let loose . . .'

Victims

- Wilfred Owen, 'Disabled'
- Mary H.J. Henderson, 'An Incident'
- Kitty Kenyon, 'A Very Heavy Ward'
- Pat Barker, *The Ghost Road*

First person voices

- Thomas Hardy, 'Channel Firing'
- Rudyard Kipling, 'A Dead Statesman'
- Wilfred Owen, 'Strange Meeting'

2 Write the introduction to a booklet of poems containing poems by one of the early voices, one of the individual War poets (Sassoon, Owen, *et al*), and one of the other voices.

Imagine that this will be the reader's first encounter with the work of each poet. Introduce her or him to each poet's work, referring specifically to one poem by each. Compare the poets' attitudes to the War and their poetic styles.

3 The poems of Rupert Brooke can be sickly and cloying for modern taste, rather too emotional and unquestioningly patriotic.

Imagine a dialogue between Rupert Brooke and either Siegfried Sassoon or Wilfred Owen. What would they say about each other's work? What might they admire and dislike? Use examples from specific poems as the basis for a dialogue between the two writers.

4 Just as fiction has a variety of genres, such as crime writing, science fiction, romance or horror, so does poetry. Try to find an example of a poem in this collection which partly matches each definition listed below. Because many of the

poets were experimenting with poetic forms, it is likely that you will find hints of the different genres in various poems – but few will fully match the definitions. Compare your findings with others in your group.

- **Narrative poem** a poem which tells a story, or describes a sequence of events.

- **Lyric poem** originally a poem sung to a lyre (guitar-like instrument). Now it refers to a poem which expresses a poet's feelings and ideas, often based on a single observation or experience.

- **Sonnet** a fourteen-line poem. It has different forms but one of its key ingredients is a sense of development: the last six lines, or final two lines, contrast with or develop the ideas of the earlier parts. Traditionally the content is personal – an account of the writer's emotional state.

- **Pastoral** traditionally a poem which depicts nature in a sentimental way (e.g. the weather is always fine; shepherds' work is always idealised, and so on). Some War poets used the pastoral poem as the basis of their work – but changed readers' expectations.

- **Epic** a long poem which deals with matters of major importance – such as the destruction of civilisation.

- **Georgian poetry** poetry which is now frequently dis-missed as sentimental or sickly – full of heroic emotions, and predictable images of nature.

- **Imagist poetry** less concerned with telling a story or describing emotions, this genre tries to capture pictures of the world in startling or memorable ways.

[5] Look at these comments about different War poets' work.
Which do you most agree with and disagree with? Working in
a small group, use each comment as the starting point for a
debate, and find evidence from each poet to support your
opinions.

- 'Siegfried Sassoon is the most angry of all the poets. His
language is therefore the most aggressive.'

- 'Isaac Rosenberg's poetry is the most difficult, on first reading,
to understand.'

- 'Wilfred Owen is the most "poetic" of the writers. His work
is sometimes spoilt by using alliteration (repetition of initial
sounds) and rather contrived (obvious) rhymes.'

- 'Edmund Blunden's poetry feels the most old-fashioned, as
if it belongs to an earlier period.'

[6] The traditional view of war poetry has been that it shows a
brutal male-dominated world. Look again at the women's
voices represented in this collection on page 62. Discuss what
view they have of the War, and how their poetry adds to our
overall understanding of the human experience of the First
World War.

[7] How do the voices of overseas poets (page 71) add to our
understanding of the War? Do the poems feel noticeably different from those written by English writers? Do their percep-
tions of the War feel any different?

Choose three poems from overseas and use them to discuss
these questions.

[8] Choose two texts in this collection which might be considered 'propaganda'. Discuss how they try to persuade their
readers to adopt a certain viewpoint. Look, in particular, at
the ways in which they use language in an emotional way.

9. Compare one non-fiction piece of personal writing with one of the fictional accounts of the War. How do they differ? We might expect the non-fiction:

- to be less literary
- to use more direct language
- to place more emphasis on content than style
- even to be clumsy in expression in places.

But this is a stereotyped view of the difference between the two forms. Use your analysis to note more genuine similarities and differences in the two texts.

Social and historical context

1. *Voices of the Great War* does not set out to be a history book. But its subject-matter is deeply rooted in a specific human experience.

From the different texts you have read, make a list of some of the factual information you have learnt about the First World War, using a chart like the one below. Then, based on this information, discuss in pairs or small groups any ways in which your attitude to the War has changed as a result of your reading.

Poetry	Non-fiction texts	Fiction texts

2. Choose the writer you have found most interesting in this selection. Find out more about her/his life, how their background has influenced the writing and how the writer's life changed with the outbreak of the War.

Present your research to the rest of the class through a brief talk or display, or write it up as a factual article.

3. Based on the different texts you have read, imagine yourself in the First World War. Write a letter home from the trenches in which you try to convey:

- a sense of the atmosphere
- the feelings and attitudes of the people around you
- your own feelings about the War.

4. The events of the First World War are now three generations in the past. How would you communicate the realities of the War to a young audience?

Using the texts from this collection, put together a small booklet or wall display which informs your audience about the War. Use quotations from various texts, plus any photographic material, to give a powerful flavour of the conditions at the time.

5. In his poem 'MCMXIV', Philip Larkin concludes, 'Never such innocence again.' This is a recurring theme in texts about the period. The impact of the War on everything – attitudes, faith, language – was so massive that Britain became a different place.

Using the Introduction on page vii and any of the texts you have read, write down some key words to illustrate this contrast, using a table like the one opposite. Some examples are done for you.

KEY WORDS	
Before	**After**
sunshine	mud
smiles	

Then you could take ideas and quotations about 1914 and produce a poster which shows how it changed people's attitudes. Part of the poster should illustrate 'the world before War'; the other half the War itself. Use key words, quotations from a variety of texts, and images to show a changed world.

6 Laurence Binyon's poem 'The Fallen' is probably the most quoted of all First World War poetry (closely followed by Rupert Brooke's 'The Soldier', perhaps).

In a group discuss which text from this collection you would be most likely to recommend as an epigraph for the War – a kind of textual monument to remind people of what the War was like. Give reasons to support your choice.

Drama and media activities

1 Choose some of the 'characters' who appear in this collection – Michael Weir from **Birdsong**, Kitty Kenyon from 'A Very Heavy Ward', Billy Prior from **The Ghost Road**, or one of the featured poets. Imagine you are interviewing her or him about the experiences of the War. In pairs, put together a three-minute interview or chat show. You could either improvise it or script it.

2 Look again at Philip Larkin's poem 'MCMXIV'. Use it as the basis of the following situation.

Imagine someone who, in 1914, signs up for service in the army, full of enthusiasm, idealism and hope. Improvise or write a monologue to show their feelings at this point. Then cut to four years later. How has the character changed? What has he learnt? How have his attitudes altered? Create the second part of the monologue or interview. Then perform the piece to the class, either live or on video or tape.

3   Put together a five-minute radio documentary for young people about the First World War. Use some of the following devices and techniques:

- a narrator to link the programme together
- eyewitnesses from the War describing what they saw, in verse or prose
- readings of poems or other texts
- music and sound effects
- interviews with writers or eyewitnesses
- an interview with an elderly person you may know who has memories of the War.

Root your ideas in the texts in this anthology – quote them directly where you wish. Aim to create a powerful and honest picture of life during the First World War for an audience unfamiliar with the topic.

4   Look back at Thomas Hardy's poem 'The Dead and the Living One', which takes the form of a dialogue. Working in a group of three, create a dramatic version of the poem. One of you should be the dead lover; one the living one; one the dead soldier's ghost.

5   Look again at Wilfred Owen's poem 'Disabled'. What thoughts and feelings are going through the mind of the soldier as he returns home? Interview him about his experiences and emotions.

6 The Introduction to this collection on page vii gives a brief outline of the development of the early part of the War – from the bright euphoria of 1914 to the disillusionment which many felt by 1916.

Working in a group of four, create a sound performance which traces the development of the War. Use a narrator to give historical details; another voice to read brief extracts from poems; another to bring parts of the fiction and non-fiction texts together. Try to create an aural version of this anthology, so that listeners gain a powerful sense of what the experiences of the First World War might have been like.

7 Choose one writer of the First World War and write a web page for the Internet. Give a flavour of the writer's life and some sample extracts to show her/his work. Write a brief account at the end saying why you have chosen the specific pieces. Aim to write a total of around 300 words. Set it out as you would a worldwide web site.

Study questions

1 Write a personal response to the writing of the First World War that you have read in this collection. Describe what you have learnt about the War itself – its history and conditions – and then describe in detail three texts which have made a particular impact upon you.

2 From the texts included in this collection, choose five that you would include in a small pamphlet called 'Literature of the Great War', aimed at new readers. Write an introduction to your choices, giving a brief flavour of the historical context, and then a specific account of what each text is about, its style, and why you selected it.

3 You read this comment in a newspaper:

> *'I really cannot see why students are asked to study poetry of a war that's best forgotten. It has no relevance to us today, and the poetry should be quietly abandoned.'*

Write your letter of reply in about 300 words, explaining what you see as the relevance of the literature of the First World War, and why you think students should continue to study it.

4 One of the challenges of studying the First World War is how we can keep its memory fresh and alive for new generations.

Imagine you have been asked to prepare a school assembly for Armistice Day – 11 November – and you wish to give students a powerful, memorable taste of the realities of the War. Using extracts from the texts and the Introduction on page vii, plus your own running commentary, write your assembly script. It might include other voices reading, or extracts of music or films. You will need to specify these clearly in your script.

At the end, write a paragraph, describing what you have tried to achieve, the techniques you have used, and how well you think the end-result works.

5 Imagine you are a soldier in the trenches. Write a letter home describing conditions around you. What are your hopes and fears? You might start: 'My dearest Mother, Thank you for your recent letter which I received this morning . . .'

6 'Siegfried Sassoon's poetry is more bitter and more angry than Wilfred Owen's.' Do you agree with this statement?

Write an essay which explores it, using quotations from two or three poems by each writer to support your point of view.

7　From your reading of **Voices of the Great War** how does poetry and prose shape the experience of war differently? Which poems seem to you particularly powerful – and communicate something which could only be said through poetry? Which prose texts are especially effective, again saying something that would only work in the form of prose? Try to explain why this might be.

8　Write a comparison of two poems and two prose texts, bringing out the particular strengths of their form.

9　Is it possible to study writers of the Great War without studying the social and historical background? Do you have to know about the War to appreciate the literature – or are the texts self-standing, speaking to us so directly that we don't need to know of their contexts?

Write an essay saying how far you have found knowing about the background useful.

10　Write your own war poem, either about life in the First World War, or about your response to some of the texts you have read. Aim to write something brief, concentrated and precise. Then write a commentary describing the decisions you made in writing the poem; how you chose your subject matter; how you changed different drafts of the poem; particular words, phrases, images or lines you are pleased with; how well you think the poem works overall.

11　Using poems and non-fiction texts, write about the female response to the Great War. What view of the War do you gain from the accounts of front-line nurses, for example, and from some of the female poets? Why do you think their work has tended to be neglected in the past?

12 Write about the role of women in the Great War, and how many of their lives were altered as a result. Start with their historical role, based on letters or diaries, and then move on to examine three of the poems by women contained in this collection.

Suggestions for further reading and comparison

Poetry

There are dozens of First World War poetry collections available. You might start by choosing the *individual poet* you have most enjoyed reading and exploring more of his work.

Rupert Brooke, The Poetical Works
Siegfried Sassoon, The War Poems
A Choice of Kipling's Verse edited by T.S. Eliot
The Poems of Wilfred Owen edited by Jon Stallworthy
Isaac Rosenberg, The Collected Works
Edmund Blunden Selected Poems edited by Robyn Marsack

Of the many collections of War poetry the following are especially recommended:

The Penguin Book of First World War Poetry edited by
  Jon Silkin
Up the Line to Death: The War Poets 1914–1918 edited by
  Brian Gardner
The War Poets edited by Robert Giddings
**Scars Upon My Heart: Women's Poetry & Verse of
  the First World War** edited by Catherine Reilly
Never Such Innocence edited by Martin Stephen

Non-fiction

The First World War edited by A.J.P. Taylor
A very readable, concentrated history of the War.

They Called it Passchendaele, 1914, Somme and **The Roses of No-Man's-Land** by Lyn Macdonald
Exceptionally interesting, vivid accounts of the War, full of diaries and letters from the people who were there.

Goodbye to all That by Robert Graves
Memoirs of a Fox-Hunting Man by Siegfried Sassoon
Two autobiographical accounts of lives deeply affected by the coming of the War.

Fiction

Strange Meeting by Susan Hill
A haunting tale of powerful friendship amid the horror of the trenches.

Birdsong by Sebastian Faulks
A deeply moving account of Stephen Wraysford, who drifts into the War unprepared for its horrors. It contains fascinating accounts of the work of miners, tunnelling deep underneath enemy lines.

Wider reading assignments

1. Choose one War poet whose work you particularly admire and write an introduction to his poetry for a new reader. Illustrate your essay with reference to four to six poems. You might mention:

   - the poet's background
   - his early work
   - how the poetry develops

- his attitude to war
- the way he uses language
- what you particularly admire about the writing.

2. Compile your own slim anthology of poems from the First World War, built around one of the following themes:

- the horror of war
- friendship
- mixed emotions.

Then write an introduction to your collection, discussing how you compiled it and why you chose the poems you did.

3. Compare two of the poets of the Great War. You might mention:

- the conditions in which they wrote
- their different attitudes to the War
- how the language of their poetry differs
- which, overall, you prefer.

4. Read some of the non-fiction titles which deal with memories of the Great War. Based on your reading, imagine what it was like to be:

- a soldier at war
- a nurse on the front line
- someone at home waiting for news.

Write a first-person account of a key moment in your life – such as the night before a battle, the evening of a battle, or receiving terrible news in a letter.

5 How do fiction and non-fiction texts tell the story of the War differently? Choose a text in each category and compare the way they both:

- capture the details of war
- organise the information
- provoke an emotional response in the reader
- tell the story of the War.

Pearson Education Limited
Edinburgh Gate, Harlow,
Essex, CM20 2JE, England
and Associated companies throughout the world.

This educational edition first published 1997
Sixth impression 2005

Editorial material set in 10/12 point Gill Sans
Printed in Malaysia, CLP

ISBN 0 582 29248 4

The publisher's policy is to use paper manufactured from
sustainable forests.

Cover design by Nina Davis

Consultant: Geoff Barton

Acknowledgements

We are grateful to the Imperial War Museum and E.T. Archive for permission
to reproduce the selection of photographs on pages 117–125 and the painting
on page 122.

We are grateful to the following for permission to reproduce copyright material:

Arnoldo Mondadori Editore S.p.A. for the poem 'Brothers' by Giuseppe Ungaretti © Arnoldo Mondadori Editore, Milano; Paul Berry, the literary executor for Vera Brittain, for the poem 'Perhaps —' from *Verses of a V.A.D.* (Erskine Macdonald, 1918 and the Imperial War Museum, 1995); Carcanet Press Ltd for the poems 'The Zonnebeke Road', 'Third Ypres', 'The Ancre at Hamel: Afterwards' and '1916 Seen from 1921' from *Edmund Blunden Selected Poems* (ed.) Robyn Marsack (1982); the author's agent for the poem 'Easter Monday' by Eleanor Farjeon from *First and Second Love* (Open University Press); the translator, Michael Hamburger, for 'Grodek' from *George Trakl: A Profile* edited by Frank Graziano (Logbridge-Rhodes, Durango, Colorado and Carcanet Press, Manchester, 1984); HarperCollins Publishers for the poems 'Battlefield' by August Stramm and 'Relief' by Charles Vildrac from *Modern German Poetry 1910–1960* (ed) Michael Hamburger (1963); the author's agent for an extract from *Strange Meeting* by Susan Hill (Penguin Books) copyright © Susan Hill 1971, 1989. All rights reserved; the author's agent on behalf of the National Trust for Places of Historic Interest or Natural Beauty for the poems 'Gethsemene', 'A Song in Storm', 'Mesopotamia'. 'The Verdicts' and 'A Dead Statesman' from *Verse* by Rudyard Kipling (Hodder & Stoughton, 1940); Macmillan for the poems 'Channel Firing', 'Men Who March Away', 'The Dead and the Living One' and 'A New Year's Eve in War Time' from *The Complete Poems of Thomas Hardy* (Papermac); David McDuff and Jon Silkin, translators of the poem 'A White Low Sun' by Marina Tsvetayeva from *The Penguin Book of First World War Poetry* (ed.) Jon Silkin, (Penguin, 1st ed. 1979, 2nd ed. 1981); Penguin Books for an extract from *The Ghost Road* by Pat Barker (Viking 1995) © Pat Barker 1995; Random House UK Ltd for an extract from *Birdsong* by Sebastian Faulks (Vintage); George T. Sassoon for the poems 'A Night Attack', 'Twelve Months After', 'Does It Matter?', 'The General', 'The Dug-Out', and 'Aftermath' from *The War Poems* by Siegfried Sassoon (ed.) Rupert Hart-Davis (1983); Elizabeth Barnett, literary executor, for 'Conscientious Objector' by Edna St Vincent Millay from *Collected Poems* (HarperCollins). Copyright © 1934, 1962 by Edna St Vincent Millay and Norma Millay Ellis. All rights reserved.

We have been unable to trace the copyright holders of the poems 'Falling Leaves' by Margaret Postgate Cole from *Poems* (George Allen and Unwin, 1918), 'A Memory' by Margaret Sackville from *Scars Upon My Heart* (ed.) Catherine Reilly (Virago, 1981) and 'Lamplight' by May Wedderburn Cannan from *In War Time* (Blackwell, 1917), and would appreciate any information which would enable us to do so.

Special thanks to Bryan Palin for his help in preparing this collection.